AMAZING SAINTS

By Phil Saint

LOGOS INTERNATIONAL

PLAINFIELD, NEW JERSEY

1972

To Ruth,

My charming wife, who has been a faithful
and loving companion during all the busy
years covered in this book.

AMAZING SAINTS
© 1972 by
Logos International
Plainfield, New Jersey
07060

Printed in the United States of America
Library of Congress Catalog Card Number: 71–124480
SBN 912106–24–7

Contents

Preface
Though the Mountains Shake
(Psa. 46:3)

I was sitting in an old, unpainted frame house in Osorno, Chile, writing a letter. It was three o'clock in the afternoon, May 21, 1960. In a rocking chair across the room an old man recovering from a heart attack sat staring out of the window. As I slipped the letter into an envelope, a hanging electric light bulb began to swing ever so slightly. I felt a vibration as if a heavy truck were passing in the street below.

All at once the room reeled. Dishes cascaded from the shelves, and pictures swayed crazily on the walls. I staggered across the heaving, buckling floor to the side of the old man. He was struggling desperately to his feet, his eyes filled with terror. Together we fought our way to the stairwell. We stumbled down it, expecting the old house timbers to collapse and crush us; they groaned and shuddered, but we got to the patio unhurt.

Above the rumble that came from the depths of the tortured earth, and the intermittent sounds of falling masonry, we could hear people screaming and moaning. One man, trying to escape from his tottering house, saw the pavement suddenly open gaping jaws and swallow his wife and baby. The fissure closed instantly, stifling the woman's desperate cry. They were gone forever.

A teenage girl ran past us, shrieking mindlessly. Three small children huddled wide-eyed against their mother, who knelt amid the rubble in the street, praying to the Virgin. A black-hatted rancher holding a dead child in his arms muttered, "All I have

lived for, over the last thirty years—wiped out in five seconds!"
The only world these Chileans knew was disintegrating.

Incredible geologic pressures, miles deep in the earth's crust,
had suddenly broken loose; and the mighty Andes Range was riding them like a gaucho on a wild stallion. Along the cordillera,
eleven volcanoes, dormant for centuries, suddenly spewed out
fiery masses of rock. Immense columns of black smoke and steam
towered up thirty thousand feet, gradually spreading in a pall
high above the green hills. Landslides buried whole villages and
dammed rivers, changing the face of the land. From the sea, vast
tidal waves, due to reach even to Japan and Alaska, raced shore-
ward, sweeping in over doomed towns, leaving boats large and
small perched impossibly atop the coastal hills. Water-logged
corpses lay amidst the tangled debris.

When the worst tremors had passed, I ran down the street, my
heart in my mouth, praying God to spare the hundreds of Christians in a nearby church where Sunday school had been in progress.

The first shock waves had struck the building while Francisco
Bilbao, the great Chilean lyric tenor, was singing. Dave Hanson,
North American guest organist, was playing a large, old-fashioned, boxlike pipe organ, and when it began to sway he thought
at first that the boy pumping the bellows had gotten too enthusi-
astic. When the pipes began crashing noisily to the floor on either
side, he looked around to see the congregation heading for the
exits.

The pastor begged the people not to climb out of the windows,
but ignoring the pleading, one old man scrambled out of a window and was crushed to death by the falling facade of the church.
As I reached the scene, men were removing the last of the cinder
blocks from his body. Blood was oozing from his lips. Pressing
my ear to his chest, I could hear soft, bubbling sounds that told of
lungs punctured by broken ribs.

That same evening, in the stadium where I was to have

preached in the closing rally of our city-wide campaign, unearthly silence reigned. The broken piano lay on its back among heavy timbers that had crashed from the ceiling. All was dark.

A more terrifying darkness lay over the stupefied minds of Osorno's survivors. All their familiar life-patterns had been swallowed up by the monster from below. Here and there small knots of people clustered around battery-operated radios—their only means of knowing what was happening in other parts of their stricken country.

Two days later we boarded a rescue plane with other refugees, flew below a heavy bank of cloud, zigzagged dangerously up a long valley between the precipitous hills, and finally landed at a larger airport. From there we flew north in one of the huge United States' rescue transports that had been sent to the disaster area.

A week later, the hideous experience of the quake seemed almost like a bad dream; but the recollection of God's presence, steadying and sustaining us through it all, was very real. Letters coming in from pastors who had taken part in our Osorno campaign reported packed church meetings, with badly shaken men and women seeking Christ. Some congregations had literally doubled. God had delivered a sermon, not from any man-made pulpit, but from the bowels of the earth; and His Word was being heeded.

I had no inkling at this time that God, Who had brought revival out of Chile's agony, would one day change my own spiritual horizons with a profound upheaval, and remake my neat, complacent little world. His plan for me lay hidden, like the forces deep below Chile's mountains; and its roots reached back into the lives of the vital, creative people who gave me life and helped to shape me.

1.

The Roots and the Buds
(Job 14:8-9)

In the days when Pittsburgh, Pennsylvania, was a bustling pioneer town at the confluence of the Susquehanna and Monongahela, a boy once traced the likeness of a river captain who plied the Ohio River in his flatbottomed stern-wheeler. Drawing with his finger in the wood dust that clung to the wall of a sawmill, the boy outlined the big-nosed, bull-bearded captain so ably that a passing businessman was ready to send the young "cartoonist" to Paris for a European art education. He soon found out, however, that the lad's father—the subject of the drawing—was a rich old coot who could easily pay for his son's education but wouldn't. So the matter was dropped.

The boy was J. A. Saint, my grandfather. He never did get a formal art education. He just drew and painted until he became a master of landscape painting, silhouette cutting, or whatever art form struck his fancy. Grandfather Saint, with his enchanting tales of the wild frontier, had the wholehearted admiration of all the Saint kids, and we cared little that his earning capacity was scant and unreliable.

We listened with rapt attention as this medium-sized, twinkle-eyed artist recounted fabulous tales of the Far West. Of course, anything west of Pittsburgh in Grandpa's day was fabulous—a

1

land of Indians, log cabins, and squirrel-shooting woodsmen wearing buckskin.

Grandpa was as versatile in art as he was in storytelling. He could imitate a Corot or a Rembrandt to perfection, and he could paint an old millrace with such skill that the water seemed to be flowing. He was a silhouette cutter of well-deserved fame, going to all the old-time expositions, where he set up his little booth, with the catchy sign, "Your Face Cut Without Pain!" His sharp little scissors moved fast, sometimes doing just the head, sometimes outlining the entire figure of a wasp-waisted Gibson Girl with a sweeping egret-plumed hat. With his black derby and big cigar, this dapper artist was a dramatic addition to any fair.

After a time the cigar disappeared. He told me how he had tried for years to get rid of the smoking habit—tried everything. With a twinkle in his sparkling blue eyes, he added, "Then I tried prayer, *and that did it!*"

I never saw Grandpa J. A. Saint angry, or even outwardly disturbed; but Aunt Hazel, his only daughter, told me that once when her brother Jim sassed his father back, Grandpa took him by the shirtfront and pinned him to the wall. There was fire in J. A.'s eyes as he measured out his words: "Don't - you - ever - talk - like - that - again!" And Jim never did.

My other grandfather died when I was about six years old. I remember him as a remote, almost superhuman personage; but even from that distance his insistence on ordered living got through to us children. We lived in a cottage that Grandfather Proctor had built behind his own large, almost palatial home in Wyncote, Pennsylvania, outside of Philadelphia. At that time we were an unpredictable tribe of five boys and a tomboy sister. Later we were eight, seven boys and a girl.

Every rake and shovel had *Josiah K. Proctor* burned neatly into the handle. The long chicken house was kept with the scrupulous care that would have suited a Dutch housewife. The grass was always close cut and trimmed with painful attention to detail by a mustachioed Italian immigrant. Grandfather Proctor could well afford these things, for he was a successful businessman, an inventive genius, and founder of the large Proctor and Schwartz Company of Philadelphia.

Thus while Dad, the son of a self-taught, peripatetic artist, was selling newspapers on the street, Mother and her sister Jane grew up surrounded by Victorian elegance. "K-Ma," as we later nicknamed Mother, attended Wellesley College near Boston with other elite young ladies of the New England area. Although schooled in all the cultured proprieties of the day, she became the forerunner of today's campus revolutionaries.

Young ladies of the time all wore tight whalebone corsets to give them tiny, hourglass waists. Those instruments of torture made it nearly impossible to breathe. Mama, convinced that the custom was both stupid and harmful, threw her corset out with the rubbish.

One can imagine how alarmed Wellesley's sedate faculty members were to have one of their students appear with a normal waist *in public!* But although strong pressure was exerted, K-Ma's stubbornness was immovable. Her waist stayed "natural."

Little by little, under the many-sided attack against the Bible at Wellesley, Mother lost her faith in the things of God. She seldom went to church, and her enthusiasm turned to writing, poetry, and art.

The extent of her spiritual loss began to come home to her when a gentleman on a streetcar asked her if she were a Christian. Indignantly she told him, "Yes!" But the question had gotten under her skin. A fellow student's tragedy affected her more profoundly. This girl had slipped a note under Katherine Proctor's door when she was out. It read: "I came to you for help, but you were not at home." Before K-Ma got back, her visitor had drowned herself in the Wellesley River.

The day after K-Ma arrived home after graduation, she heard Ralph Connor, author of *The Sky Pilot,* speak in the Wyncote Presbyterian Church. In the middle of his lecture, he pointed directly at Mother and asked, "Young lady, are you doing what you know God wants you to do?"

At the end of the lecture, Mother made a beeline for him. "Sir," she said, "I know that I ought to be serving God and my fellowmen, but I have no faith. I haven't anything to offer those in need. What must I do?"

With the wisdom which comes from living in the Spirit, Ralph Connor replied, "There is a verse of scripture which applies to your case. It is John 7:17." He turned to it and read the words of Jesus: "If any man will do His will, he shall know of the doctrine, whether it be of God, or whether I speak of myself."

As Mother listened, her large gray eyes intent upon him, he went on: "Young lady, the Lord Jesus says that if you are *willing* to do God's will, you will *know* if what He taught was the truth or not."

Mother went to her room, knelt by her bed in the darkness, and said, "Oh, God, I am willing to be shown. I want to know."

The Holy Spirit responded with a miracle. Faith came to her like a flood. She knew!

The next day she went to an Italian mission and made arrangements to teach there. In teaching, her faith was greatly strengthened.

Then K-Ma fell in love with a young man destined to be one of the great poets of the century who was tutoring her at home. Although returning Katherine's affection, Ezra Pound stubbornly refused to accept her Lord. He said flatly that God's will would not be allowed to interfere with his life.

K-Ma's reply was equally definite: she must break off their relationship.

"You can't do it!" Pound exclaimed. "You love me too much."

"But I can," she replied, "because, much as I love you, I love the Lord more."

Preferring his own will to the Lord's, Pound went on to poetic fame. But during World War II, while living in Italy, he turned traitor to his country. Brought to trial in the United States for this capital offense, he pleaded insanity; and instead of being executed, he was placed in a mental institution.

Later K-Ma and my brother Dave visited him in the asylum where K-Ma was able to talk to him about the Lord. Eventually, Pound was released and returned to Italy.

To complete the curious circumstance, while Dad was an art student, and before he met my mother, he dated a non-Christian poetess named Hilda Doolittle. He broke with her because of the claims of Jesus Christ on his life. Years later, in Italy, Hilda Doolittle became Ezra Pound's lover!

Dad had quit school after the fourth grade, and had gone to work. When finally he was able to attend the Academy of Fine Arts in Philadelphia, he still had to work in an art studio for a living six months of the year, working on stained glass. The other six months he spent in art school, living in a garret under a tin roof, broiling in summer and freezing in winter. Philadelphia was strange to him, but hardships were not, and his consuming desire was to become a great artist. He was learning to sketch accurately with charcoal, to paint with skill in oils, and to acquire the rich techniques of contemporary great masters. Distinguished artists of that day felt a sacred responsibility to train students who showed especial promise. Redfield, brilliant painter of snowy landscapes, was among these, as well as Daniel Garber, who could capture the glorious colors of an old quarry or autumn trees beside a forest stream.

Young, thin, and threadbare, Dad was a most unimpressive figure; but how he painted!—the whole gamut of art. There was one exception: he would not paint from the female nude. Fellow students, notably those of the loose-living French school with their ribald jokes and Bohemian parties, soon caught on that Dad was a "square." One day some pranksters informed Dad that from then on he would have to draw from the female nude and like it, or else! Dad defied them, and was carried bodily into the classroom, where they dropped him at the feet of a completely disrobed woman model. Dad kept his eyes closed. Released, he got to his feet, looked his tormentors in the eye, and said (perhaps a bit pompously), "Gentlemen: principle in art as in other things!" Then he walked out.

Earlier, you see, Dad had sat under inspired preaching. Dwight L. Moody, the bushy-bearded, stout shoe-clerk-turned-evangelist, was shaking two continents for God.

Later, converted under the ministry of that great orator, Dr. J. Wilbur Chapman, Dad became a fiery witness for Christ, trying to convert everybody within reach. Once his sister Hazel found him sitting astride his younger brother Jim, holding him down until Jim finally promised to read his Bible every day—a promise he faithfully kept throughout a long and busy life as a banker.

Dad's radiant Christianity directly challenged the easy morals of his fellows at the grand old Academy of Fine Arts; and his stand against carnality threatened to cost him a prized traveling scholarship to Europe, the mecca of all worshipers of the fine arts. Dad worshiped only God; yet he wanted to go overseas so badly that he dreamed about it at night and tasted it with his food. The difficulty was that, among various types of art work, he must present a drawing of the female nude; and of course he steadfastly refused to do this. At the last minute, however, the Academy's governing board made a special ruling, permitting Lawrence Saint to submit a portrait instead.

God honored his stand for purity, and Dad won a traveling

scholarship to Europe's great art centers. His ambition was to be a great portrait painter, but God had other plans for him. One day, as he stood in the dim nave of an old cathedral, drinking in the heavenly beauties of its ancient stained-glass windows, tears of rapture began coursing down his cheeks. He knew in that moment that God was calling him to his life's work—to revive this inspired medieval art in glorious colored glass.

Demanding as it was, Dad's devotion to art did not keep him from attending evangelistic meetings at the Young Men's Christian Association in Philadelphia. And the love of Christ burning in his heart led him through the filthy slums to the same rescue mission where pretty Katherine Proctor was trying to instruct little bootblacks and pickpockets in the Word of God. Very shortly, Dad found himself keeping the disorderly, small ragamuffins in control, while the prim young lady taught them.

The college-educated heiress to Proctor wealth may have been perturbed by the young artist's occasional mistakes in grammar, but his radiant spirit and his unusual talent drew her strongly. When Dad went back to western Pennsylvania for the summer months, he stored his paintings in Katherine's elegant home.

When Dad won his next scholarship to Europe, Katherine asked to go along. Dad said she oughtn't to consider such a thing unless they were married, and he added what his father had told him, that a man should never plan on marrying until he had saved a thousand dollars.

Katherine said, "My aunt has left me a thousand dollars. Why can't we use that?"

So, on June 10, 1910, there was a hurried wedding in the downstairs salon of the Proctor mansion. K-Ma had made her own wedding dress, in such fashion that it would be suitable for traveling; and since her parents had planned a trip to Oberammergau at that time, they took the newlyweds partway.

In France K-Ma spent her honeymoon climbing scaffoldings

and standing on rickety ladders high up in the great dim cathedrals, holding her artist-husband's paints while he copied the ageless, stained-glass windows.

Lawrence's original paintings were secured by the Victoria and Albert Museum in London. Later, he was commissioned to make copies for the Carnegie Institute of Technology, in Pittsburgh. His published study, *Stained Glass of the Middle Ages,* is still the master work in that field.

Some years later, when Dad was on his way to recovery from a seven-year illness that had kept him bedridden most of the time, a courteous stranger stopped at his seat in a railway coach. "Sir," he said, with evident feeling, "your resemblance to the portraits of Christ is so strong that I felt I must ask your name and occupation."

"I'm Lawrence Saint," Father replied, "and I make stained-glass windows."

The stranger smiled more warmly. "My name is Pitcairn," he said, "and I am building a cathedral. I should like you to work for me."

Dad, somewhat startled by this offer, explained that he was not yet recovered from a very serious operation and could not work; but Raymond Pitcairn finally persuaded him to put in a few hours a day. Dad served as a stained-glass designer in the Pitcairn studio for eleven years; and his windows in the Bryn Athyn Cathedral outside of Philadelphia are still seen by a continual flow of art lovers.

In after years, commissioned to make windows for the National Cathedral at Mt. St. Albans, in the nation's capital, Dad conceived a daring project: he would learn to make his own stained glass, following medieval recipes. "Experts" declared that these wouldn't work, even if they could possibly be translated from the ancient French; but Mother went to the library and did the difficult translations.

Dad had already experimented with his own recipes for colored glass. The first time that he believed he had succeeded, he joyfully called the family out to see his triumph. We all trooped eagerly into the studio, and looked; but there was no stained glass to be found—until some one accidentally stuck a finger into a sticky mess and asked what it was. The "glass" had melted—a wrong mixture!

The ancient French formulas, however, were successful. Following them, Dad made his own glass in quantity. One recipe called for shavings from a cow's hoof, so Dad asked the local butcher for the raw material.

"No problem!" the butcher answered him; and the next day on his way to work he tossed a cow's leg, hoof and all, into the yard.

Another recipe called for cuttings of human hair. Our town's barber was glad to offer sweepings from his floor. Another formula needed a potato, to take the bubbles out of the glass. Dad's first potato was too big, and made the hot glass spatter all over everything.

One day Dad returned to his studio to find that the forty-foot window that he had set up in wax had collapsed. The sun had melted the wax. Dad went back into the house and wept: "A whole year's work—gone! Ruined!"

Mother went out alone to see the "wreckage." She returned with the incredible news that none of the glass was broken. It could all be reset.

Dad and Mother were not at home the day fire swept the studio. Sam, who was man-grown and a member of the volunteer fire company, was talking with me in my bedroom-studio when the fire alarm sounded. He tore down the stairs and charged out of the front door at full gallop, hoping to be first at the engine house so he could drive the big red fire truck.

Once outside, he saw the flames and rushed back into the house, shouting, "It's Dad's studio!" We snatched several glass-bottle fire extinguishers from their wall brackets and dashed out to do battle with the roaring flames. I hurled an extinguisher through a window so hard that it sailed clean through the building and out of the opposite window, to land unbroken in the mud of our neighbor's truck garden.

The fire engine arrived and brought the fire under control, but the whole interior was black and gutted. A few hours later, Dad returned from a short trip to find a year's work reduced to bits of shattered glass and melted lead.

Not long before Dad's studio burned, he had had a strong impression to move his masterpiece, the Last Judgment Rose Window, to the cathedral, and had done so. However, he did not remove three smaller windows depicting Moses in different aspects of his life. These were burned and completely destroyed. In the remaking, they were much improved. I recall that the staff of workers took over all available space in our home when they used it as a temporary studio.

To the end of his life, Dad felt that bringing Bible subjects to life in stained glass was a sacred calling, and that it demanded his total, passionate devotion. Mother learned that when Lawrence was caught up in creative fervor, ordinary routines of living must be set aside.

In later years people often called Dad "Dr. Saint," chiefly because of the distinguished-looking beard which had first drawn Mr. Pitcairn's attention. It was flame red when he was young; afterward it turned snow-white and was clipped to a point, in the Vandyke style.

The home that my parents made for their fast-growing family was noisy, haphazard, carefree—and wonderful! The house was for the kids, not the kids for the house. We played on, scrambled under, and climbed over everything in the place. Floors were scuffed, walls marred, and windows were broken at times; but we lived to the full.

I recall vividly some of our very few visits to the immaculate, orderly Proctor mansion. While the womenfolk were in the kitchen preparing lunch, we boys were having a hilarious time in the sedate parlor with its imported Persian rugs and highly polished floor. We were tearing at full gallop across the room, jumping onto the overstuffed Davenport, and catapulting through the large bay window onto pillows on the porch. We were whooping and shouting like Indians on the warpath—when the regal, massive figure of grandmother Proctor came sweeping into the room like an aircraft carrier steaming majestically into harbor—and all the steam suddenly went out of our play!

Sam was the eldest. I came second. Mother once told me that I'd been born in a hurry in the living room by the front door. "And," she added in her matter-of-fact New England way, "you have been in a hurry ever since." She recalled that I'd had colic for six months, and hadn't stopped crying the whole time. "Even then," she asserted, "the Lord was strengthening your lungs and your vocal cords for preaching."

When we were little, Mother tried to practice on us some of the child psychology she had studied in college. But while she was anxiously fluttering through the pages of a book on *How to Reason with a Small Child,* Dad was applying the primitive and effective measures taught in the Bible. In plain King James English, it says: "Withhold not correction from a child: for if thou beatest him with the rod he shall not die. [It often sounds like it, though!] Thou shalt beat him with the rod and shalt save his soul from hell" (Prov. 23:13–14).

Whenever we were stubborn or rebellious we were punished; and when we did well we always got an affectionate pat on the head. Mother soon caught on, and, whenever Father was not on hand, proved well able to chastise us.

We were all about two years apart, and always together. When we went to church, we looked like an orphanage trooping in, filling an entire pew. Any boy who gave signs of "acting up" was made to sit beside Father; and real trouble awaited anyone who caused a commotion in church! I remember one time when I had the "honored" spot next to Dad. He looked down at me with a fond smile and said, "Son, maybe someday you will be a preacher."

I said nothing; but I recall poignantly how my little heart froze within me. I said to myself, "That's the last thing in the world I ever want to be!"

Sister Rachel was the darling of our Proctor grandparents and of other family friends. She was often invited to spend a week or two away from home. We boys were somewhat jealous of her, since no grown-ups in their right minds would ever invite *us* anywhere. This, along with natural brother-and-sister antagonism, inspired a name for her that didn't make a lick of sense: "Boochel and Company Witchhazel."

When Rachel found herself hopelessly outnumbered, she would take off up the steep back stairway, like a cat up a tree; then, darting into the bathroom, she would bolt the door. No one guessed that, even then, Rachel was being toughened up for the mission field.

Many years later, Sis wrote from Mexico, saying that she was at a missionary boot camp of the Wycliffe Bible Translators, learning to drive mules. I wrote back to her, "Driving mules ought to be a cinch for one who was raised with seven brothers!"

Of course, God had planned all of our upbringing from infancy through our teens with the future in mind. Before sending Sis to the mission field, He brought her under the deeply spiritual influence of Addison Raws and his consecrated staff at the Keswick Colony of Mercy in New Jersey. This was a Christian center for the rehabilitation of alcoholics.

Rachel's training at the Keswick Colony and Bible Conference

Center gave her a missionary's one indispensable piece of equipment: a Spirit-led life. With this to develop her natural poise and courage, she would be prepared to win continuing victories through Christ.

2.

Growing Pains

Huntingdon Valley, where we moved from Wyncote, had one main street, two side streets, a general store, a barbershop, a bank, and little else. The countryside was a fairy-tale land of rolling grainfields, woods, and babbling streams. Country roads meandered past old gristmills and quiet farms. Sometimes they plunged into the echoing plank tunnel of a covered bridge. Pale, spotted buttonwood trunks accented the dark tones of cedars and pines; and through the huge tulip poplars floated the bell-like notes of the wood thrush. Beyond the trees, open fields were splashed with daisies and yellow buttercups. Violets carpeted certain sheltered nooks.

I remember the hillsides dotted with black and white Holstein cattle—and the lilting flight of swallows which nested under the eaves of dairy barns. Our parents let us run free within wholesome limits, trusting the Lord to take care of us since it was impossible to keep track of so many children all the time.

I don't remember hearing of anybody drowning in the swimming hole at the Pennypack Creek, but it was well over our heads, and a lifeguard was unheard of. In winter the dangers multiplied. We skated all the way from the dam at the waterworks to the rapids by the old mill. Many times the ice was half-melted, and there were open spots. Of course, we boys had to test the strength of the ice around these holes, trying to see who could get nearest to the open water without breaking through. Now and then one of us fell in and had to be fished out.

We tried everything. In summer we made skis of barrel staves, using a well-soaped ladder for a ski chute. Slap-slap-slap! The barrel staves clattered down from rung to rung, inviting broken arms and legs. Once I, the runt of the family, and skinny, outdared my brothers by crossing from one tree to another, swaying perilously on slender branches.

Despite the dire predictions of two old-maid neighbors, we all survived, to invent more breakneck stunts.

Keeping Sunday afternoon holy was a big problem for Dad, who truly believed that it was the Lord's Day and should not be turned into a worldly holiday. Our forenoon, of course, was taken up with Sunday school and morning worship. In the evening we attended Christian Endeavor and the evangelistic service. The afternoon hours were when steam pressure built up in eight lively youngsters.

On balmy Sunday afternoons Dad often took us for long walks, which we always loved. We stopped among the trees by the creek to skip stones over its mirrorlike water. We teetered like would-be acrobats on high fence rails. Once in a while we chased a frightened cottontail rabbit. In season we found big red oxheart cherries in the trees along the dusty roads, and in the fields, wild strawberries.

These excursions were a lot less strenuous than our weekday romps—jumping and tumbling in the haymow, trapping in the woods, fishing in the old quarry, flying our kites in a swooping, snatching wind. Dad always encouraged do-it-yourself activities. Between Sundays he took time to help us make swings, wagons, "roller-coasters," and scooters; and on a rainy Sabbath he would often seat us on either side of a long table he had made from old piano panels, and give us Bible scenes to color with crayons. He had outlined the scenes and printed copies of them on his gelatin hectograph. They might show Adam and Eve being driven out of the Garden of Eden, or the story of Cain and Abel, or any of the New Testament parables. Noah and the Ark, with all the animals, and the Great Flood were exciting subjects.

Dad, like Grandfather J. A., was a master storyteller. He could describe, with every imaginable sound effect, how David slew Goliath, Daniel in the lions' den, and Joseph in Egypt. But the best-loved story of all was about the day when Jesus died. We clustered around Dad, fascinated by each dramatic tone and gesture, some of us on his knees, others on the floor.

Once in a while, for a special treat, we would pile into the antique electric car, which formerly had conveyed the Proctor grandparents through town with slow but stately grace. This ponderous relic was loaded with lead batteries fore and aft. It had windows all around, and two cut-glass vases inside for flowers. Silken tassels swaying elegantly and rather uselessly gave the interior a regal air. Dad, the driver, sat in the back lefthand corner, working the steering bar. To go left, you pushed it; to go right, you pulled it toward your stomach. Fortunately, Dad was not too fat, or he would never have made the corner!

When the car faced a steep grade, we all had to get out and walk up. We usually beat our dauntless old conveyance to the top because it had to zig-zag to cut down the climbing angle. There was little danger of meeting another car. Motor vehicles were so few on country roads in the early 1920's that dogs and children could safely lie on a sun-warmed, black-top pavement. We kids did just that when we were chilled from staying too long in the old swimming hole.

There was an unforgettable afternoon when Sammy tried to garage the electric car all by himself. Dad wasn't home, and Mama wasn't in sight. Once in the driver's seat, little Sammy pushed the hand lever all the way forward, and the drive wheels began to turn. Slowly the old relic gained momentum. As it neared the barn, Sam pushed the steering bar away from him to do a left turn into the doorway. He made it, then suddenly realized that he had to stop. He grabbed the hand lever—too low— and the car's forward movement reversed! The solid rubber tires gripped. With motor whirring, the car lunged back out at an angle, and struck and snapped a post that supported the corner of the shed. The crashing roof just missed our old juggernaut, which broke through the fence and came to an ignominious stop, its wheels sinking down into the mud of our neighbor's truck garden. This was hardly a promising start for a pilot who would one day be flying monster 747 planes across the continent with more than three hundred and fifty passengers on board!

I recall other Sunday afternoons, when the weather kept us in, and the kitchen hummed with animated family discussions, while K-Ma prepared heaping platters of food for her hungry crew. (Believe it or not, we used twelve quarts of milk a day!) The discussions covered everything that came to mind. Right and wrong emerged clear-cut; black and white never blended into gray. The Bible's counsel was our criterion, and our spiritual welfare was always on Dad's mind.

Our thorough schooling in right and wrong did not always keep us from a slip; but we had a family altar, with Bible readings and prayer every day. Sometimes interruptions threatened to overwhelm it, but Dad's persistence was amazing. He refused to give up. This daily time of meeting with God remained, a spiritual bulwark for every one of us. To this day I cannot recall the specific moment when I was converted, but by the time I was five years old I knew that I loved Jesus and that He had truly saved me.

All the children had to go to cottage prayer services. These were held in old-fashioned parlors, with dim kerosene lamps and the portraits of grim, bewhiskered ancestors staring down at us from the walls. There was usually a foot-pedal organ wheezing the opening bars of a hymn with the voices of the old folks joining in. Scripture reading, a time of prayer, and a simple exhortation followed. We were the only children there, and we weren't always listening; but the spiritual atmosphere soaked into us, and some of it remained.

Dad, with inspired insight, understood this, and had an inflexible rule that anybody too tired for prayer meeting was too tired for play and must go straight to bed. He knew that some of the faith and grace of those old saints was communicable, even to restless kids.

Deacon Gray, of the Methodist chapel, lived just across from the cow pasture on Red Lion Road. Deacon Gray always knelt when he prayed. He prayed softly, without hurry, and one could sense about him the presence of angel wings. We knew he was face-to-face with his Lord, and when this dear old man walked down the street, we felt that he walked with God. In Wesleyan terms, he had experienced the anointing of the Holy Ghost.

God's power was at work in all these impressions. Once we received a visit from smiling, white-haired Dr. Howard Kelly, one of the three founders of Johns Hopkins University and Hospital. He and a number of his friends had come to see how Dad made stained-glass windows. We young ones gathered around him like puppies around their dinner dish, listening eagerly as he talked about his experiments with snakes, insects, and other creatures. A thing that especially fascinated us was a beautiful red rose in the buttonhole of his lapel. It never faded, even after hours in the hot summer sun. At last one of us worked up the courage to ask him how it could be real and still keep so fresh.

Turning back his lapel, Dr. Kelly showed us the tiny glass bottle of water attached to the stem. "My flower has a secret source of life," he explained. Then he went on to say that he himself had a secret source of life—Jesus Christ the Lord.

The fact that this outstanding scientist owed every grateful hour of his life to the Son of God was more convincing to us children than any memorized statement of faith. Yet many of these early impressions lay buried and partly dormant through my growing teens and maturing years, until a profound spiritual upheaval brought them up to the light.

I was still a teenager when God raised up a fiery young seminary student by the name of Percy Crawford. His preaching stirred me mightily, as it did thousands of other young people. While working his way through a fundamentalist Presbyterian seminary, Percy had been assigned to an abandoned church in an old, run-down part of the city. Not satisfied with a routine ministry, he formed a male quartet and soon had a radio program. Then he began holding youth rallies, which shortly developed into a series of evangelistic campaigns. He set up an evening Bible school and a bookstore. Next, he bought a bankrupt hotel in the Pocono Mountains and opened a Bible conference there. I was one of the first young volunteers to help clean up the dilapidated place, and was also the first lifeguard and dishwasher.

Two of us ran the wheezy old dishwashing machine. Steamy vapor poured out of it, and sweat poured down from our bodies. One day, George, a tall, bronzed, athletic type, threw down his towel in disgust. "I quit!" he declared, and stalked out. It could be coincidence, but as far as I know he never appeared in Christian work again. Believing that I was working for God and not for man, I stuck it out. Privileged, some years later, to preach and draw at that same Bible conference,* I was grateful for the days when I had proved "faithful in little"—even washing dishes.

During that earlier period, my contacts were not all Christian.

* Pine Brook Bible Conference.

Some of my high school companions were quite unregenerate. On the other hand, the "dates" I chose were all Christian girls— with one unforgettable exception . . .

An attractive, teenaged girl was the pianist at a seaside resort where I was vacationing. I had no trouble whatever in getting a date with her, though she had never seen me before. Innocently, I thought her readiness rather flattering. I had much to learn.

On the night of our date, almost as my car pulled away from the curb, she moved up very close to me. She produced a comb from her purse and began mischievously combing my hair. Her intentions were obvious; and for a moment I was almost over- whelmed by the intoxicating nearness of her physical charms. Then my home training broke the spell, like throwing a switch. Greatly upset, I drove around the block, reached over and opened the door on her side.

"This is where you get out," I blurted.

She looked at me as if I were out of my mind; then it dawned on her that I was serious, and she got out. She had, so to speak, tried to breach the wall of an invisible fortress—a godly family life. It is no accident that my six brothers all married fine Chris- tian girls, and have stayed happily married to them.

Percy Crawford strongly reinforced all the bulwarks of my home life. He brought into his conference men who preached the necessity of surrendering completely to God, so that His Spirit might take possession of each human faculty. This preaching broke some time-hallowed ritual patterns, but we teenagers loved it. Percy organized Bible clubs, which usually met in private homes. Here the holy scriptures glowed with warmth. They radi- ated a power seldom felt in formal church services. We were en- couraged to give spontaneous personal testimonies to the work of Christ in our hearts and lives. In these spiritual confrontations I saw clearly the Lord's claim on my life although at first I resisted.

There was the night when I took a youth delegation to hear a special conference speaker, a Canadian named Albert Hughes. He was a short man with a nose like the keel of a sailboat, and a message like a battle flag. At first I listened with smug approval, thinking, "All right, preacher, give it to them! These young people need it!" Then, little by little, the Spirit of God working through Dr. Hughes began to show *me* what a poor Christian *I* was—compromising with worldliness while posing as an example to other young believers. The Word of God, wielded so ably by the speaker, was like a sledgehammer, demolishing all my self-esteem.

My guilty mind conjured up the smutty vaudeville shows I had attended so often on Saturday nights with my foulmouthed companions. I never swore, and seldom if ever told an off-color story; but I ran with the crowd that did. Sitting there under Dr. Hughes' impassioned oratory, I slumped lower in my seat. Scene after scene came vividly to mind—the comedian telling his filthy sex jokes, the provocative dancing of the chorus girls, and the films I had seen depicting so much that was sensual and brutal!

God was showing me the shallowness of my life, so filled with church activities, yet so devoid of Christ. When Dr. Hughes challenged us to come forward, I knew I ought to respond; it was time to clear the slate. But like a typical teenager I wondered, "What will the gang think?"

My conscience retorted, "You're a coward!"

The altar rail was filling up with earnest young people when I was finally ready to step out. Two fat women were blocking my way to the aisle on one side, and on the other were several members of the basketball team I played on. I could just hear these fellows giving me the "horselaugh" afterward: "Did you see Saint going up there tonight? What a dope, falling for that emotional stuff!"

But God was shaking the very depths of my soul. Blinded by hot tears, and not caring now what anybody else said or did, I somehow reached the aisle. At the altar rail I dropped to my knees and sobbed, "Lord, if You'll keep me busy, I'll serve You till I die!" (And indeed He *has* kept me busy from that day to this.)

I knew I was choosing between Christ and self, between total commitment and going through empty motions. Yet, now that the choice was made, I had no clear idea of what I was going to do for the Lord. I had some thought of drawing religious cartoons for some evangelical magazine, like E. J. Pace of the *Sunday School Times*. Becoming a Christian chalk artist or a preacher or a missionary never once entered my head. I just wanted to do something of eternal value, *for Him.*

With youthful enthusiasm I went to the altar on several other occasions; and then, at Pine Brook Bible Conference, I ran into a spiritual block. God had put His finger on a lie that I had told when I was only six years old.

My mind recreated the scene with painful clarity—the ropes of a high swing that Dad had hung from a big poplar tree behind our house, the ground falling steeply away below it, and my younger brother Dan and I, swinging separately, each on a rope, after the seat had been untied. We swung to dizzy heights, in opposite directions, and inevitably we collided. Dan fell, landing on a rock that broke his leg. When the ambulance arrived with its siren wailing, I was out of sight under the porch, crying and trembling with the knowledge that it was all my fault.

Asked about it later, I declared that Dan was to blame, because he had swung out last. This was a lie. And now, years later, God's "still, small voice" told me to set the record straight.

"But, Lord," I argued, "everyone has forgotten about it. Besides, I was just a child."

The voice of conscience was implacable. "Straighten it out!"

So I did. Humbled, I wrote a letter to my parents confessing my lie. Perhaps it was a small thing; but I was learning that God wants everybody who serves Him to purify himself, "even as He is pure" (I John 3:3).

The inward struggles continued. There were moments when I resisted His reshaping of my mind, and there were some temporary defeats. One beautiful June day I was sketching in a cow pasture, drawing a picture of an old stone springhouse shaded by spreading maple trees. It was shaping up well on my board when a little neighbor girl, about eight years old, came running across the sunlit field to see what I was sketching. As she sat watching me work, the Holy Spirit nudged my thoughts.

"Speak to this child," He seemed to be saying. "Tell her how to be saved."

Minutes passed as I groped for courage. I waited for what I thought would be a proper opening to broach the subject, but it never came. I never got to the point. No doubt my foolish pride was to blame. At any rate, the little girl's mother called her, and she went running across the daisy-dotted field, leaving me desolated by my failure.

Months later, the little girl suddenly took sick and died. For weeks I felt deep remorse, convinced that her blood was upon my soul. I pictured her as lost because I had failed to obey the voice of the Holy Spirit. Only the Lord and I know how greatly relieved I was finally to hear that this sweet child had found Christ as her Savior at the little Methodist church, just before she was taken ill. I had learned a hard lesson.

God kept speaking urgently to my heart about such matters, but I remained backward and shy. Often I threw myself across my bed, shaken by uncontrollable sobs, because I could not bring myself to tell more people, person-to-person, about my Savior and theirs.

At this same period, my family was caught in the battle between "fundamentalism" and "modernism." The so-called higher criticism, spreading from intellectual centers in Germany and elsewhere, attacked the authority of the Bible. It even questioned the existence of Jesus of Nazareth in history. Sometimes the enemies of holy scripture were sneaky; again, they were loud and bold. On all fronts they were testing the quality of Christianity in the Protestant world. They won many shallow church members to their way of thinking, and confused many more. Preachers in every major denomination began openly or secretly to doubt the accuracy of the Bible, and therefore its divine inspiration.

On the other hand, great scholars like Dr. J. Gresham Machen of Princeton, and a minority of able preachers, were standing firmly against this tide of untruth. Among them was Pastor Ballback of the Bethany Baptist Church at Fox Chase, three miles from our home. When we Saints began attending there, we escaped for good the poisonous tendrils of doubt. Pastor Ballback thundered out against ungodliness in all its forms, and he preached with the power of Christian love. He showed us clearly that there could be no compromise with those who denied the miraculous life of Jesus Christ our Lord.

From the services in our former church, our family used to come away discouraged and full of futile arguments. From the Bethany Baptist Church we came home blessed and fed. Dad was soon appointed deacon, and he spent the last years of his life in happy fellowship with true men and women of God, remaining an active soul-winner to the end.

For me, the real greatness of Father's life is not so much in his works of sacred art as in his passionate desire to lead men to Christ. Mother fully shared this desire with him. A part of their reward was living to see three of their eight children become missionaries (one of these a martyr) one other a faithful pastor, and all truly converted Christians.

3.

The Urge to Draw

People have remarked that, with my militant Christian background, it is no wonder I became a missionary; but they've usually added the question, "But what led you to combine preaching with *art?*"

The answer is that I've always liked to draw. Dad taught me the fundamentals of art, with patience and devotion that I would not have met in any art school. He was a hard taskmaster. Sometimes, when I had labored all day over a picture, he would study it carefully, tell me I could do better, and send me back to my drawing board to start all over again. Mother was quick to sense when I got discouraged—and just as quick to tell me that my sketch was "wonderful." My high school teacher, Mrs. Blanche Williams, also spurred my will to improve. But one day Dad made a nearly tragic discovery: I was partly color-blind!

He checked me with panels of stained glass, and proved beyond question that the only one of his sons who showed promise of following his honored profession could not distinguish half the colors of the spectrum. "From now on," he counseled sadly, "you must work only in black and white—charcoal, pen and ink, and pencil."

For some time I followed Dad's advice; but several years later, when I began to illustrate my sermons with crude sketches in chalk, I *had* to use colors. Furthermore, I liked cartooning! Even if I'd not been partly color-blind, Dad's stained-glass art was far too slow for me.

When Dad learned of my interest in chalk work, he was heart-broken. He thought it a quick, cheap device which would keep me from mastering any fine art. His reaction hit me hard; but I couldn't drop this tool I believed God had given me to serve Him with. I let Dad know that I would rather do rough chalk sketches and win souls with them, than create masterpieces and win fame. Besides, I pointed out, Dad had a friend from Academy days who was a gifted portrait painter and who worked *fast*. His name was Willard Ortlip, he came from a Free Methodist family.

In his student days, Willard Ortlip had been a very worldly young man, and this was a heavy burden on the heart of his Wesleyan Methodist father. The senior Ortlip prayed every day, at a certain hour, for his wayward son. One day, as he was praying, he felt God's definite assurance that the boy would be saved. A few days later a letter came from Willard, telling how he had received Christ as his Savior and Lord.

Young Willard had a Jewish sweetheart. When the girl asked him what Christians believed about Jesus Christ, Willard told her accurately what his godly father, a Methodist lay-preacher, believed. Deeply impressed, the young lady asked for a copy of the New Testament. She read it avidly, and received the Savior into her heart. With His Divine help, she then converted Willard! Dad used the faces of both the Ortlips in his stained-glass representation of the Prodigal Son.

About this time, a visit to the Ortlips opened to me new spiritual and cultural vistas. Our whole family was invited, for Willard had remained in touch with Dad ever since Academy days, and their friendship had grown steadily warmer. In our host's comfortable, rambling home on the Palisades overlooking the Hudson River, I sat entranced watching this great artist paint. His work was magnificent. Later I studied the many canvases stacked in his studio, some of which had won prizes. I admired Mrs. Ortlip's fantastically beautiful floral paintings, and saw that she was as gifted as her husband.

What amazed me even more was learning that Mr. Ortlip would often take his easel and chalks to some street corner in New York City, and draw Bible scenes for the passersby! As he drew, he would preach, urging men to be reconciled to God. He always said in his preaching that Jesus saves, keeps, and *sanctifies!* He emphasized that God could, and did, heal the body as well as the soul.

Between the Ortlips and Dad there lay an obvious difference in doctrinal emphasis. Willard's meetings were "noisier," less formal than ours; yet it was clear that he and Dad had a very high regard for each other, both as artists and as Christians.

After this visit, when I heard that Ortlip was to draw at a camp meeting on Long Island, I made it a point to be there. I sat spellbound that afternoon, watching him draw Christ before Pilate. There was magic in the way he created the scene—Roman soldiers, principal figures, architecture, and all—in fifteen minutes! The gospel preaching was excellent; but the altar call upset me. Everybody seemed to be praying aloud at the same time!

This was foreign to all I had been taught about proper worship; yet I was struck by the difference between this huge crowd's enthusiasm and the almost apathetic behavior of many in the churches I was used to. Here, when the meeting was over, nobody wanted to go home. I couldn't help contrasting these happy faces with the solemn looks of other congregations I had known.

Of course, Dad agreed with the Ortlips that God works miracles of physical as well as spiritual healing today; but his attitude at that time lacked the enthusiasm of his friends' belief. He may have sensed that Willard's intense enthusiasm could well magnify the actual healings that took place.

Once Dad took us to the Bible Institute on the Hudson River which is now Nyack Missionary College. There students prayed for the sick just as naturally as they prayed for anything else. Again, I recall a saintly man of prayer who had an orphanage and a home for old folks at Warminster, Pennsylvania, not far from where we lived. He looked like a prophet right out of the Old Testament, and he interceded for people who needed physical help. The healings which occurred in evident answer to his prayers were real, beyond any doubt. But these matters were out on the fringes of our spiritual awareness.

Our Bible teachers insisted that the unusual healings and miraculous gifts of the Holy Spirit that had characterized New Testament times were meant for that period only, not for us today. They told us that we were to be satisfied with the salvation of the soul, and thereafter with steady spiritual growth. Any special spiritual "baptism" or "anointing" for service was taboo. They put forward what seemed to be scriptural grounds for their stand, and I had no urge then to question it.

While Willard Ortlip's example did little to dispel my religious prejudices, his amazing chalk work gave me real inspiration. It showed me what great possibilities my chosen medium held. However, it was well for my first attempts at drawing in public that I had no critical audience.

During my initial summer at Pine Brook Bible Conference, the head of the Sunday school department at Bethany Baptist Church, Miss Elsie B. Sutton, asked me to draw for an assembly of juvenile classes. Her letter mentioned that she had seen some of my illustrations in a young people's paper. What she could not have known was how much her invitation would mean to me, or the qualms with which I would accept it.

A week before the great event, I rummaged around in Dad's studio and found a rickety old tripod which threatened to collapse at a touch. I bought a ten-cent box of blackboard chalks at the nearby general store; and for drawing paper I tried dry-cleaner bags cut in half and turned inside out. Of course, the chalk was too hard and the surface of the paper too slick, but it was all I could find.

That Sunday, standing before the wriggling, nine-to-twelve-year-old youngsters, I struggled through the half-hour period. First I explained to them what I was going to draw; then I drew it. Afterward I told them what I had drawn, hoping that it made sense to them! Earnestly I told them how to be saved. In my great desire to win them to Christ, I forgot my panicky feelings, and God made up for what I lacked in eloquence. One of the boys who received Christ in that first meeting later became a Baptist preacher. That morning, he described my "special program" to his father with such enthusiasm that the father asked me to give the same program for the men's Bible class.

When I graduated from high school, Dad took me to see Herbert Johnson, a famous cartoonist, who had a big estate just a few miles out of town. Out of friendship for my father, Mr. Johnson promised me a job as secretary-chauffeur and general handyman —on the condition that I go first to business college.

To business college I went, for eight months. It was a new world to me, with its hundreds of clattering typewriters, its stress on machinelike accuracy and speed, but I soon became used to that. But I could never get used to the salacious talk of some students. One disreputable youth in particular was so foulmouthed that nearly every sentence was a dirty joke, or else laced with profanity. The thought came to me more than once that I ought to tell him about the Savior of men, but I believed that he was beyond all hope of being saved.

Several years afterward, in a gospel meeting, a face across the aisle from me riveted my attention. I knew I should recognize it, yet I couldn't. When the service was over, I introduced myself. "I know I've met you somewhere," I said.

"Of course you have," he replied, smiling. "At Strayer's Business College."

"But—you're not *that* fellow?"

"Yes," he assured me, laughing, "the same—with a big difference."

He went on to say that after business college he had gone to work, then lost his job because of his rotten way of life. He'd drifted from place to place and finally got work driving a milk wagon. A Christian lady on his route had begun talking to him about her faith and giving him tracts. He threw the first tracts away, but they kept appearing, and at last he started to read them. Little by little, through her vibrant faith, the housewife broke through his hard shell. In the end she persuaded him to attend an evangelistic campaign, and he was soundly converted.

After we parted that evening, I said to myself, over and over again, "If God could save that man, He could save *anybody!*"

From business college I went straight to my promised job with Herbert Johnson. I commuted daily from home in my antique Model-T Ford, often returning through town driving the boss's long, sleek limousine. The pay was meager—twelve dollars a week—but the glory, oh, the glory! of driving the big car and of watching the great artist work every day—that was all that counted. At first!

Herbert Johnson drew weekly cartoons for the *Saturday Evening Post*, besides doing some advertising cartoons for a thousand dollars each. I believe he was the highest-paid cartoonist in the country at that time. His draftsmanship was fabulous. The dramatic expressions that he got in the faces he drew, and the action in his figures, were incredible. They were also hilariously funny and served as mighty missiles to land his political opinions on target. Each week I carried the cartoons to Independence Square, where the Curtis Publishing Company was located.

The *Post* ran little cartoons, sprinkled through its pages, and these challenged me to draw one. The idea came to me full-blown. It showed a western miner hightailing it for the hills in silent panic, while his bewhiskered partner, with a magnifying glass, was trying to light a fire—unaware of the huge bear behind him blocking out the sun. The gag line was, "Hey, Bill, get outa the light!"

The humor editor to whom I handed it looked at my "masterpiece" very soberly, then tossed it on a pile with some other offerings. My hopes crashed. I didn't know then that humor editors never laugh at cartoons. But later I found opportunities to ask in the engraving department if they had seen a cartoon about a bear.

"Yeah," said one of the men, "I seen one de odder day."

Feverishly I began leafing through the thick pile of proofs stuck on a long prong on the wall. About halfway through I found a bear cartoon—but it wasn't mine! When the engraver saw it, he said, "Dere's anodder one." I looked further, and, sure enough, there was a proof of mine. Jubilee! I was famous—with a cartoon in the *Saturday Evening Post*! And the thirty dollars I eventually got for it seemed like a fortune.

For six months I drove my artist-employer's big car, typed letters, and did whatever else was needed. When a drought threatened to kill all of the hundred or more newly planted pine trees on the Johnson estate, he pressed me into service with hoses and buckets of water. After a long hard day in the broiling sun, I came up with a better idea. Why not call for the fire truck, run a hose line to the pond, and water all the trees in jig time? I asked my boss about it.

Johnson telephoned, and the volunteer firemen came. They watered all the trees in a matter of minutes, and almost washed some of them out of the ground!

The many important, and even famous, people who came to visit my employer gave me an overall picture of what material success, wealth, leisure, and creature comforts can do for human nature; and the picture brought certain scripture verses into sharp, new focus, for example, this saying of King Solomon: ". . . I gathered me also silver and gold . . . And whatsoever mine eyes desired I kept not from them. I withheld not my heart from any joy . . . and behold, all was vanity and vexation of spirit" (Eccles. 2:8, 10–11). I recalled the words of Jesus: "What shall it profit a man if he shall gain the whole world and lose his own soul?" and Paul's observation: "She that liveth in pleasure is dead while she liveth" (Mark 8:36; I Tim.5:6). I saw one wealthy woman often, but in six months' time I never saw her smile. In contrast stood my own family, practically strangers to this world's wealth, yet secure in the love, joy, and peace that only Christ can give.

My employment with the great cartoonist ended suddenly, when I broke my right arm cranking the rusty old Model-T. You might call it the ancient Ford's dying kick, since I was about to drive it to the junkyard. Johnson would willingly have kept me on, after my arm healed, as chauffeur, pupil, and factotum, but I took the injury as a sign from the Lord. I was certain, by now, of God's plan for my life: to draw souls to Christ through chalk art. And this would take all of my time.

Telling Mr. Johnson was not easy, because I knew his impatience with my "extreme religious views"; but somehow I got the words out. Predictably, this man of downright opinions blew up.

"You'll be wasting your time! You're crazy to run around drawing pictures for farmers in country churches." He ranted on, until I fled from the storm, a badly shaken young man.

Years later, after a thrilling meeting in a large city church, a distinguished-looking gentleman came up to shake my hand and to say, "More power to you, Philip! Keep up the good work." It was Herbert Johnson!

But now, coincident with my injury, K-Ma's seemingly endless endurance had played out. A long rest was prescribed. And so, with my arm in a sling, I crossed the continent with Mother to New Mexico.

We soon located an old adobe ranch house, twenty miles from the drowsy cow town of Alamogordo, and only a few miles from what later became White Sands Atomic Proving Ground. There Mother sat for hours in the warm sunshine, reading her Bible or drinking in the wild beauty of the Sacramento Mountains as their soft pastel colors changed from hour to hour.

Looking back, now, I wonder how Mother ever carried on through the long, hard years when we children were growing up—years when Dad was too ill to work steadily, and was often sick in bed. Yet she gallantly kept up with her endless chores, raising eight lively youngsters, nursing us through measles, scarlet fever, chicken pox, and flu. She infused us all with her spirit and courage, even when she was on the ragged verge of collapse.

Our school clothes were often threadbare. I wore my elder brother's hand-me-downs. In the class photograph, taken in front of the grammar school, I sat cross-legged on the ground in the front row, wearing short pants and ugly black cotton stockings, my hands trying vainly to cover two big holes in the knees. Mother had been just too exhausted to mend them.

Now, in the sunlit desert air, she was getting tanned to a deep Indian brown and was growing visibly stronger. This thrilled me more than the whole six months of riding horses in the "wild west."

I don't know how the rest of our family managed for all that time without K-Ma; but everyone's joy was tremendous when she returned home with the old sparkle back again in her eyes. Mother lived for her family, but, more than that, she shared our individual enthusiasms and encouraged each of us to try new ventures. When my elder brother Sam, a senior in high school, suddenly decided to take flight training without waiting to graduate, Mother instantly backed him up. With the same wise and warm understanding, Mother encouraged me to continue giving chalk talks in Sunday schools, young people's meetings, church services, and finally in evangelistic campaigns. Her faith in us was no passive sentiment; she always found ways to translate it into action.

Airplanes were Sam's meat and drink. He had traded many hours of grease-monkey work for short flights with Ernie Buehl, the "Flying Dutchman." When his longing for a pilot's license could bear no more delay, Mother understood. She made some heroic readjustments in the family budget, and sent Sam off to an air school in St. Louis. Later, with his license secured, he quickly finished high school and went on to engineering studies at Drexel Institute of Technology.

There at Drexel, the faith in which his parents had reared him, gave Sam courage to rebuke an atheistic professor before a class of two hundred students. "Professor," he declared, "what you have been saying about Christ has nothing to do with this course in English. You have no right to make such blasphemous, filthy statements. I wish to go on record as saying that I believe Jesus Christ to be God's Son!"

Sam thought he might be expelled for his boldness, but he wasn't. Afterward a member of the class told him, "Saint, I'm a Jew, and I don't believe as you do in Jesus Christ; but I would like to say that I admire your stand."

Thirty-odd years later, another member of that class, now a distinguished atomic scientist, wrote to my sister Rachel: "At that time I wouldn't have had the interest or the courage (to back Sam up); but that classroom experience was the beginning of my search for truth. I determined to find out for myself, and studied all the religions—Buddhism, Mohammedanism, etc.—and I also read the Bible. I decided that Christianity was the truth and that it had the answers I sought for."

Sam was not the only one interested in flying. Little tow-headed Nate, number seven of the Saint "tribe" was beginning to glue up model airplanes and take old clocks apart, about the time that his oldest brother went off to flight school. Nate, even as a child, shared Sam's strong spiritual convictions; but nobody ever dreamed that "Thanny" (short for Nathanael) would one day become a daring bush pilot in the jungles of South America.

In those early years, we took K-Ma's intense belief in us for granted, and there is no doubt that its fruit was our deepened loyalty to the principles she stood for. Her strength, her enthusiasm, became ours.

Dad was slower to accept my calling to chalk-art evangelism. When I was just beginning, he asked, with some anxiety, "Son, what are you going to be, a preacher or an artist?"

"I'm going to be both," I replied, and this did nothing to allay Dad's doubts. He was present at one meeting to watch my crude easel work. After the service, he came to me, much disturbed.

"What color did you intend to use for the sky?" he asked.

"Why, powder blue, of course," I answered.

"Son," he said, shaking his head, "you used a loud, raw, *turquoise green!*"

From then on I kept "loud, raw, turquoise green" out of my chalk tray. (Usually, if I start a picture with each chalk in its place, and double-check in case of doubt, I get through a drawing all right. There are times, though, when I can't tell blue from purple, green from gray, or chartreuse from tan. Once, during

World War II, I did a sketch of a German soldier in a prison camp in North Carolina. I wasn't aware, until someone told me, that I'd made the face a loud *yellow-green!*)

Eventually Dad was convinced that my call to be both chalk artist and preacher was of the Lord, but he had reason for some painful doubts at the start.

The first summer camp where I was invited to speak and draw, as a young preacher-boy, was Camp Tappuah, just outside of Asheville, North Carolina. It was on the same mountain as Ben Lippen Bible Conference Center. Dr. Pierre DuBose, late president of the Hampden DuBose Academy, had somehow heard of me, and he asked me to come for a month in the summer. A month! I didn't have enough messages to last a week, but I felt led to accept the invitation by faith, and I went.

In something like desperation, I picked up a book written by a Bible teacher and tried to work out a message from each chapter; but I was soon floundering. The erudite theologian's treatise, with its philosophical approach, was simply not adaptable. After two or three attempts at fighting the Philistines while wearing Saul's armor, I discarded it, picked up the humble sling of the country boy, and chose my own ammunition—simple Bible talks. For success, I relied on the Holy Spirit.

Some of my hearers received Christ. Among others who manifested a desire to know the Lord was a little fellow about twelve years old. He was so matter-of-fact about it that I doubted if he really meant business; but the following week, back in his home at Asheville, his new life in Christ began to break through. One day his godless father left his bottle of hard "likker" in the kitchen, and the lad promptly poured it down the drain.

When the father discovered the empty bottle, he was furious. "Who poured my whiskey down the sink?" he roared like a wounded bear.

Little Johnnie stood soldier-straight, and looking up with big, solemn eyes said, "I did, Daddy. That stuff is bad. It makes you do mean things." His father stared in disbelief, but said nothing, and turning on his heel he left the kitchen.

The following Sunday night I had an evangelistic service in a nearby church, and the recently saved boy got his father to come. The man sat at the far back of the church, but at the invitation he was the first one to come forward. As I met him at the front, he said, "I don't know what's happening to me; I feel all torn up inside."

His feeling "torn up" was the beginning of his being made whole.

To one particular friend I owed a great deal in those fledgling years. He was Jack Wyrtzen, whom I had met at Percy Crawford's Bible Conference in the Poconos. Jack had been selling insurance by day and leading his own jazz band in New York nightclubs; but after the Lord saved him he promptly got into Christian work with a number of other fiery, dedicated young fellows. For greater outreach in their Brooklyn neighborhood, Jack and the boys had rented a large church auditorium for a series of four Sunday nights, but Jack had only three sermons. He reached me at home by telephone.

"Come on up," he said.

"Okay, I'll be there," I told him.

This would be my first evangelistic trip away from home. Dad insisted that I ought to stipulate my travel expenses, at least, before starting out; but I wouldn't hear of it. I was going to trust the Lord for all of my needs—a principle which I have followed over the years.

Jack's Sunday-night service was wonderful, with rousing songs, testimonies, and special music, topped off with my chalk pictures and preaching. At the invitation, some thirty people came forward. Among them were the son of the church's pastor, and his wife; also a young man, Phil Worth, who later entered the ministry.

With their fast-growing Christian outreach, Jack and his group began using the old Missionary Alliance Auditorium at Eighth Avenue and Forty-Second Street in New York. There was always a radio program, followed by a direct evangelistic appeal to those who filled the auditorium. Many came in from the crowded sidewalks of the sex-ridden Broadway theater district, and numbers of them were dramatically saved. Sailors from the ships of many nations came, and found Christ. Some of these were from Argentina—a land then far beyond the horizon of my thoughts.

One odd but happy little character who always showed up at these rallies was "Scotty" Malcolm. A hunchback, with thin, pipestem legs, he looked like a little old gnome. The narrow, piercing eyes behind his huge nose bore out the impression. Scotty made a scratchy living washing windows, and I suspected that Jack Wyrtzen was supplementing that small income. At any rate, Scotty was always rejoicing, always witnessing for the Lord.

Another outstanding witness at Jack Wyrtzen's meetings was Walt Oliver, one of the most ardent and successful soul winners I have ever known. For years he was a part of Jack's Word of Life staff; but before God saved him at a Word of Life rally, he'd been active both in politics and in church affairs. A prominent New York church was paying him fifty dollars each Sunday night to serve as emcee at a kind of religious club. At the same time, some politician friends were pressing him to run for mayor. "You're just the honest-citizen type that people will vote for," they urged.

Along with the aroma of liquor and expensive cigars, Walt smelled their greed: once they had put him in office, these "friends" would expect their cut of the "take." But that their idea attracted him was painfully clear to his wife, listening in the next room. She was a devout, praying Christian, and when Walt's friends had gone, she told him she would leave him if he threw in his lot with that crowd. When he failed to take a stand, she did leave, to stay with relatives.

Alone in his strangely empty home, Walt answered the telephone. It was his adored granddaughter, begging him to go with her to a youth rally Saturday night. "It will be wonderful, Grandpa! Please take me!"

Learning that it was a Word of Life rally, with a large youth choir, chalk pictures, and a gospel message, Walt tried to back out, but he failed. The upshot was that he found himself on Saturday night sitting with his wife and his granddaughter, six rows from the front of the packed theater. And when the invitation was given, Walt Oliver came to the platform with many others. From there he went to the after-meeting, where I saw him for the first time.

Counseling those who were giving themselves to the Lord, I said, "If you are in a church where the gospel is not preached, get out of it. Go where you will be fed on the Word of God." And Walt took this to heart. Returning to the socially eminent church where he had been active, he asked the pastor, "How is it that in all the time I've been coming here you never told me that I needed to trust in the finished work of Christ, and be born again?"

The pastor intimated that if he preached that kind of sermon he would have no overflow crowds at his services. So, Walt left, and the Lord opened up for him a very effective ministry, both public and private.

Looking back at the ramified ministry now under Jack Wyrtzen's direction—three Word of Life camps, huge youth rallies, bookstores, radio and television programs, overseas conference centers, and a Bible institute—I find it hard to believe that he was ever a green youth, just beginning his public witness for Christ. I have been with Jack in countless great rallies, and every summer at his Word of Life camps, but one night, very early in our association, stands out in sharp contrast to them all.

This evening, a quartet was to sing, on radio, with a trumpet trio coming in on the second verse. The tenor couldn't reach a certain high note, so they dropped the music down a note—forgetting to tell the trumpets. When these came blasting in on the wrong note, the number broke up!

Later, Jack went to the station director, completely crushed. The cigar-chewing man turned an understanding gaze upon him. "Don't worry about it, son. In the first place this just shows that we're all human. In the second place, nobody listens to that program, anyway."

Little did he know that one day Jack's Word of Life hour would be one of the most popular Christian broadcasts in the nation.

4.

Preacher in Love

More and more, itinerant preaching filled my days. In the next few years I crisscrossed the states, driving thousands of miles, with the burning desire to be used by my Lord in bringing lost men and women to Him. Among the miracles that I saw, of souls reborn by God's Spirit, certain ones glow with special warmth in my memory.

There was Jimmie Kron, a young linotype operator for the *Daily News*, in Jackson, Mississippi. He had been invited to my meeting by George Sugg, the city editor, who used my chalk pictures for bait. Jimmie was the sort who usually managed to get out to church on Sunday morning, if it didn't rain, or if the weather wasn't too hot. He used hard language and cherished some sinful habits, but he was a church member. Old-time salvation was far from his mind when he came into the meeting where I was to draw and preach; but the hard-hitting gospel shattered his empty profession of religion. God took command of his life, then and there. His charming wife, Floyce, came with him down the aisle, her arm in his, when the invitation was given.

Now, after more than thirty years, Jimmie represents the Gideons as he travels constantly throughout the southland. When witnessing to Jesus' power to save, he begins by saying, "On January 23, 1937, at 9:00 P.M., in the Central Presbyterian Church, I was born again and became a child of God."

When Jimmie's life was thoroughly remade, his latent abilities began to flourish. Today he is in charge of the *Daily News* production, and everywhere he goes he speaks spontaneously about his wonderful Lord. Furthermore, the quality of his life backs up every word he says.

On that same 1937 trip, in Philadelphia, Mississippi, I was thrilled by the testimony of a certain very courageous, white-haired lady whose name I never learned, but who is certainly known by the Heavenly Father. Three churches had come together for a typical evangelistic service and a great many people were present when this lady came to the front during the invitation and asked for permission to speak.

I had learned to be careful about allowing "volunteers" to address a meeting that I was conducting, but this person's evident poise and culture reassured me. With my consent, she faced that big gathering of her townspeople.

"All of you here know me," she began simply. "You know that I have been a Sunday school superintendent in this city for many years. Before tonight I had been wondering why my efforts had been so lacking in fruit, why I have had so little lasting influence with the young people under my care."

She paused, then added with evident emotion, "Tonight, for the first time in my life, I realized that I myself had never been born again."

In dazed silence the audience tried to take this in. Abashed, the pastor of her church came forward and tried hastily to cover the stark truth of her confession. But he could not hide the naked fact; a woman in the work of the Lord had not known the Lord of the work, and she had had the humility to say so! It was a lesson I would carry with me the rest of my life, one that many years later would encourage me when I was forced to admit before the world that there was a serious lack in my own life, not in regard to salvation, but related to complete victory in daily living.

Eventually I found myself running out of preaching material. In plain fact, I needed more education, and I knew it. Mother did not agree. She felt that her evangelist son would be spoiled by "higher" learning; after all, wasn't her own faith undermined when she was at college? Besides, she worried about my health. I was so thin that, with my high forehead and narrow face, I looked top-heavy in a hat. Mother declared that the strain of college studies, plus extracurricular preaching, would land me in a sanitarium for tuberculars.

"If you so much as teach a Sunday school class in college, your health will fail," she prophesied.

Frankly, I didn't want to go to college, after being seven years out of high school; but the need for it met me on every platform. One day I talked it over with Dr. Wilbur Smith, for whom I was holding some meetings just west of Philadelphia.

"Why not try it for one year?" he said. "You don't have to decide now to go all the way through." He knew very well that if I started college I would finish.

I registered at Wheaton, and at one other college, unsure which one of them God wished me to attend. At the end of August I was sharing the preaching with other staff members at Deerfoot Lodge, a rugged, Christian boys' camp in the Adirondacks. Alfred Kunz, the director, had two of his attractive daughters at Wheaton; and since Carol, the elder daughter, and her roommate needed a way to get back to school, we planned to go together. My Plymouth business coupé would just hold the three of us, with baggage, and we planned to stop overnight with my Aunt Amelia and Uncle Jim in Erie, Pennsylvania.

The morning we were to leave camp, "Uncle Al" called us into his living room for a brief period of devotions. He opened a book of daily readings by Vance Havner, entitled, *Consider Him.* The meditation appointed for that day was about Philip the Evangelist! It told how the disciple of Christ, at the command of God's angel (Acts 8:26), left his highly successful meetings in Samaria for the desert road that ran from Jerusalem to Gaza.

Vance Havner suggested that Philip may not have liked leaving a great spiritual harvest to go to a barren wilderness. He pointed out how, at times, God calls on us to take a step of faith that is against our natural inclinations. (This is exactly how I felt about leaving the work I was doing to go back to school!) God, Havner pointed out, may have in mind somebody whom He wants you to meet.

This was prophetic. It was at Wheaton College that I met my vivacious and sweet wife, Ruth Brooker. Plainly, the devotional reading for that day—the very day I was leaving—was no unplanned coincidence.

The Wheaton of 1937 caught me up in a new world of studies, friendships, and extracurricular activities. All freshmen took Bible courses under a tall, plain woman who wore her hair in a fat bun atop her head. The clothes she wore on her large frame were old-fashioned, too, but they suited her well; and in time we came to associate them with her glowing spirit.

Her teaching was truly God-inspired, and the least sensitive of us felt her personal interest, Christlike in its warmth. Her name was Miss Edith Torrey. She was the daughter of Reuben A. Torrey, who had so deeply influenced my Dad years before. I remember how disappointed she was to learn that I had no thought of becoming a missionary.

Her watchful care for our spiritual health was occasionally disconcerting. Smoking by students, on or off campus, was taboo, and the rule was so well kept that even a faint odor of tobacco smoke would have been noticed at once. One evening on campus, a Shakespearean actor was giving a monologue in which a famous passage required a candle. Coming to the edge of the platform, he asked if someone in the audience would give him a match to light it. This was probably his way of getting closer rapport with the students, but nobody moved. The actor repeated his request. None of the faculty stirred, and none of the students. The artist waited, puzzled and a bit impatient.

Just then I came to life up in the balcony overlooking one end of the platform. That afternoon I had been to a Boy Scout picnic, and I still had some big kitchen matches in my pocket. I tossed half a dozen of them onto the stage, and then—I saw Miss Torrey! She was sitting with other faculty members in the front row. She stared at those matches with horror. Slowly she swung her head around and up. Her piercing gaze swept the balcony to discover who was carrying matches, and they found and transfixed me. I knew that an "interview" was coming up! Fortunately, I was able to explain the matches to her satisfaction.

In my second term, I switched from literature to zoology, partly for the drawing it involved—crayfish, frogs, beetles, and such. I took all the art courses I could. DeWitt Whistler Jayne, then head of the art department, had done two paintings which fascinated me. They were portraits of venerable faculty members. How fluid they were! What color and what life! I absorbed all I could from DeWitt. I painted furiously. I did a mural of birds— all kinds and all sizes of birds—for the science department, and a biblical mural for the library. I was having a wonderful time!

In the middle of my senior year, the abrupt ending of a three-year-old college romance left me dazed and hurt.

One day, several months later, I stopped at the office of Dr. Alexander Grigolia, professor of anthropology.

"Well, Mr. Saint, how things are going?" he asked with that quaint European inversion of his. I knew what he meant. He had a way of guessing what was on a fellow's mind; so I confessed, "I've got a list of prospects . . ."

"Of course," I added, reddening, "they don't know anything about this yet."

Quite seriously, Dr. Grig nodded. "Tell me who they are," he said.

I named over several whom I thought to be very nice Christian girls. When I came to Ruth Brooker, Dr. Grig brightened visibly.

"Ah," he declared, "she is execkly fitted for your life. You must get her."

I didn't really know Ruth, but I caught his enthusiasm. "Tell me more, Doc, tell me more!" I begged.

I owe this brilliant scholar an eternal debt of gratitude, not only for his good advice about Ruth, but also for giving me a thorough scientific orientation that has undergirded my entire missionary career. A clear understanding of culture patterns, racial groups, and the supreme importance of adapting to new environmental situations often spells the difference between success and failure on the mission field.

It took just four dates before I was completely and wildly in love. Ruth's spirit, her sparkling humor, every adorable change of her features as she talked or listened, were all I could dream about. For a whole week I found study impossible. My body went to classes, but my mind was preoccupied—with Ruth. I waited, chaffing like a racehorse at the starting gate, for classes to finish, so that I could see her again.

Putting my feelings into words, as we sat one night on the porch swing at her home, was the hardest thing I ever tried. The setting was perfect for a proposal. Moonlight threw a pattern of shadow and silvery light around us, and a soft little breeze was rustling the rose arbor. And Ruth was so near, so quietly confident! I struggled for the right words—and gave up. Instead of proposing marriage, I just asked her to pray about it.

I was too late with that request. Ruth had already prayed, and in the library next morning as I bent over to whisper something to her, I noticed that she was making up a list of bridesmaids! I was momentarily staggered, but in fact we had already discovered that we were made for each other. Through the years I would grow daily more grateful for a wife who knew how to make vital decisions and carry on from there.

Though our courtship was brief, it could not be called hasty. I knew that Ruth was a wholly dedicated Christian, singing for Christ in gospel meetings. For her part, she knew that I was a seasoned evangelist, though still in my twenties. She had counted the cost of becoming a peripatetic preacher's wife, and she'd accepted it with the resilient spirit which would meet every challenge the years would bring.

Others were due for a shock. My future father-in-law was a dignified Englishman, London-born. Almost before he knew my name, I asked him for his daughter's hand in marriage. With true British self-control he didn't bat an eye.

"If her mother is agreed," he replied, "I will give my consent."

I turned to Mom Brooker, but she, too, "passed the buck," saying, "If Ruth is sure of her decision, it's fine with me."

Ruth and I looked at each other. She gave me the sweetest smile I had ever seen. We would be married in the fall.

The Saint family never had spent much time on ceremony. There were so many of us that birthdays were barely noticed. However, Rachel and Dad did come to my graduation. They met Ruth, who looked more like a high school girl than a college graduate; and when Rachel saw how it was between us she took me aside. She didn't quite bend my ear, but her tone had the same effect.

"Now, don't you go breaking that little girl's heart," she adjured me.

My answer was a big smile. "Don't worry," I said. That's the last thing I'm going to do." I didn't say a word right then about our being engaged; it would be fun to let Sis keep on guessing for a while.

Dad's reaction was just as positive, in a different way. Once he had talked with Ruth, he gave me his patriarchal blessing. He had a rare gift of insight that I never knew to fail. Besides that, he had decided Ruth's profile was identical with Shakespeare's—sans beard.

After graduation, Ruth and I parted for the summer. While I was back East, Mother decided to send my fiancée a silver dish with her name engraved on it. She asked me for Ruth's middle name. "Search me," I answered. "I don't know the girl that well yet."

Later in the summer Ruth paid a visit to my folks. Before she arrived, the memory of a previous, unexpected rejection shook me. Would Ruth change her mind as the other girl had done? It was a case of "A burnt child dreads the fire." But our happy meeting sweetly reassured me, and afterward, on our way back to Wheaton College with some other alumni, something happened which put an end to my last fears about Ruth changing her mind.

We made a two-day stopover at my Aunt Amelia's home, near Erie, Pennsylvania, a farm which stretched from a country road back to a river. While we were there, I impulsively offered to help with the digging for a septic tank. I worked alone for several hours; then, tired and sweaty, I went to the river to throw some cold water on myself. I had just finished when Ruth came running wildly across the fields, calling out my name with every breath. She had found my shirt and jacket lying near the deserted hole, and imagined that something terrible had happened to me.

Holding her trembling body close to mine, I knew beyond ever a doubt that she really loved me. I felt humbled and deeply comforted.

Pastor Evan Welsh married us that fall before a Wheaton student audience in the college church, the love lighting his eyes under their shaggy brows as we stood before him at the altar. He had led Ruth to the Lord at Bethany Camp on Winona Lake—

where Ruth had gone because she liked horseback riding and water skiing.

Evan Welsh was a soul winner well aware of the fact that countless young people, even those who attended church, have never heard God's simple plan of salvation. Sensing that Ruth was one of these, he had asked her, "Ruth, are you living for the Lord?" She hardly knew what he meant, but Welsh's warm friendliness had her attention; and shortly, with bowed head, she was opening her life to the Savior. Later, Pastor Welsh had the joy of leading her father, Arch Brooker, to Christ, not long before Arch died.

With the ceremony and all our well-wishers behind us, we drove that night to Three Rivers, Michigan. Since we had hidden our car in a downtown garage in Chicago, it had escaped the usual tin-can-and-old-shoe decorations. We had circumvented all of the pranksters but one—sheer fatigue. Wedding preparations on top of crowded preaching engagements had caught up with me, and my bride drove into Three Rivers at two in the morning with her groom snoring lustily beside her.

In our first year we traveled a great deal, holding meetings through the South and East. Soon our first child was on the way, and I had signed up to work in army camps with the Pocket Testament League. A war was on!

We were in the process of moving to New Jersey from my brother Sam's home in Port Washington, Long Island, when Ruth's labor pains began. She was already in New Jersey, and I was packing the last of our belongings into the car and its one-wheeled trailer when she telephoned that she was on her way to the hospital. Moments later, I, too, was on the way. Crossing the traffic-jammed streets of New York City with a heavily overloaded trailer took an eternity. When, desperate with anxiety, I arrived at the hospital, I found Ruth and her mother sitting on a bench in the hall. No bed was available until later. Tiny Ruth Ellyn joined us that night. All went well.

Next evening I was in the first meeting of a church campaign in Plainfield, New Jersey, an hour-and-a-half trip from the hospital. After the service, a telephone call was waiting for me. I was stunned to learn that our little daughter was a "blue baby" and might not live.

She did live, but with the heartbreaking condition called cystic fibrosis. Yet she was a happy child, and unusually bright. Every year that we had her to cherish was a special gift from the God she loved.

How will I ever be able to describe the action-packed days of ministry with the Pocket Testament League in the great army camps during the war? Under the able leadership of Alfred A. Kunz, affectionately known as "Chief," we were working to get the Word of God into the hands of all servicemen. The project was furthered by large-scale evangelistic meetings. Our teams were scattered all over the United States, and we ran into many difficulties, despite Chief's great tactical skill and endless patience. We suffered, along with the rest of the civilian population, from the severe gasoline and tire shortages, and the heavy traffic on trains and buses.

God chose the place for Ruth and me to make our home, in Paramus, New Jersey, just above Route Four which goes straight to the George Washington Bridge and New York City. When it was impossible to get tightly rationed gasoline, all I had to do was to get my portable easel down the stairs and across the highway in order to catch a bus.

With this in mind, I reconstructed the easel into two cases. The first case had small rubber wheels on one end and handles on the other. The second box was clamped on top of it. The combination was just narrow enough to trundle down the aisle of a bus. Sometimes several bus drivers would pass me by. The New Jersey buses did not cross the bridge, and the ones that did were too crowded for me to get on with both boxes; so I used to leave one at a newsstand, take one across, and then return for the other. I pushed the two-box combination to the subway and rode down to the Pennsylvania Station.

One day, as I was about to go through the subway turnstile, a man making change in a booth yelled at me, "Hey! You can't go on the subway with those boxes!" Hardly pausing, I replied, "Watch me, brother!"

He watched helplessly as I dropped the boxes down and wheeled them neatly under the turnstyle and onto the subway car. Of course, once I reached the first army camp, there'd be a truck to carry my equipment—and gasoline procured by the chaplains.

The League's use of special features was highly successful in attracting crowds of servicemen. Pete Boyko, later to work with me for a time in Argentina, played his golden trumpet, triple-tongueing, to the delight of the men. And Gene Palmer, a converted gambler, started out by showing his audience how he used to fleece suckers out of their paychecks. He worked clever magic tricks that kept the boys mystified, or else roaring with laughter. Gene looked like a bartender, with his high, bald dome, heavy jowls, and shaggy, black eyebrows; but when he moved from his comedy role into the thrilling account of how God turned him from suicide to the sawdust trail in a great Billy Sunday tabernacle meeting, the men always grew quiet.

When the ex-gambler finished telling his soldier audience how God rescued him from a gambler's hell, there was always a big response. Many men stepped out to confess their need of Christ and to receive Him as Savior. Gene had reached them, with language they understood.

Besides Pete Boyko and Gene Palmer, our PTL team used singers, famous athletes, and other talented people. My chalk pictures and the preaching that went with them were well received. I can never thank God enough for the privilege of ministering to thousands of men about to leave for bloody battlefields—and to the broken and wounded men who came back!

In one vast army hospital, as we went from ward to ward, a big soldier on crutches stumped along with us. He waited until near the end of each brief service, and then left. We found out that he was going ahead to each ward to herald our coming. He talked so enthusiastically about our work that everybody was prepared when we came in. Afterward he spoke to me, and with tears in his eyes, told me how much our ministry had meant to him. He was a preacher's son who had drifted away from God. He promised that from now on he would be true to the Savior Who had spoken so clearly to his heart through us.

At Fort Dix, New Jersey, we found that the chief chaplain did not want any special features. We were told to hold a straight preaching mission. He remained adamant to our objections. So for a week we put away the easel, the gambling tricks, the musical instruments, and conducted formal church services. Attendance was pitifully small—a dozen men on some nights, four or five on others, although the army chapel was built to hold several hundreds. After a week of this, we protested again to the post chaplain, insisting that we would never reach the men that way. He faced the plain fact, and gave us permission to use our special equipment.

A few hours later we were on the porch of a large assembly hall, within view of hundreds of servicemen who were wandering aimlessly about. I did some quick chalk sketching, Gene Palmer showed two or three magic tricks, and white-haired George Stephens, Southern evangelist, called out, "Come on in, men! We're going to have a great meeting!"

In five minutes the auditorium was packed to capacity, and men were peering in through the windows. At the end of the meeting, more than thirty broke out of the crowd, publicly accepting Christ.

In the army camps, we were working among tough men of the world. We prayed for power and wisdom to penetrate the barriers which had kept most of them from ever attending church. We used posters and banners with floodlights, lively march music, and stirring gospel hymns amplified by loudspeakers. We went to the mess halls to make spot announcements about our programs. And the men came.

In one camp, the chaplain refused to request for our use the large service club in his area. We were left with the day room, which would hold about thirty men. But I went to work anyway, putting up a colorful, ten-foot banner in front of the pitifully small building. A stout colonel, puffing on a big cigar, came out of headquarters just across the street, and watched for a moment.

"What are you doing, son?" he asked.

"I'm getting ready for a program we're putting on tonight, sir," I replied.

The officer removed his cigar. "Is this the same program that was put on for the troops last night?"

On hearing my affirmative he turned back to the headquarters building. "Come in here," he ordered.

I came. In thirty seconds he had captains and lieutenants hopping around that office; by eight o'clock that evening we had seven hundred men at the service club.

I always tried to be at home when our children were born. Each time, I arranged to be close by for two weeks; but somehow our babies were never punctual, and before the critical hour I always had to leave. Our second daughter, Martha, arrived two years after Ruth Ellyn. At the same time, a neighbor, Sylvia Regrut, gave birth to a baby girl for whom no feeding formula could be found. The doctors despaired of her life, but we prayed that God would spare the little one; and He answered us, so simply. Ruth began breast-feeding little Susan Regrut along with wee Martha, and both thrived.

Inevitably the work in the army camps required many trips far from home. In winter, when bitter winds were drifting snow about our house in Paramus, New Jersey, I was working in camps through the deep South. Ruth had to stoke the old-fashioned coal furnace in the basement. From time to time it went out in spite of her desperate efforts; and with two little girls in the house—one of them weakened by cystic fibrosis—its stone-cold rooms were a setting for tragedy.

Going off on trips may be a lark to those who spend most of the year enjoying the comforts of home; but traveling constantly year in and year out is something else again. There were times back in those hectic days when I felt like punching somebody in the nose, when silly, unthinking people suggested that "it must be sooo-o romantic to travel so much!" No one with a father's sense of responsibility can help but suffer, knowing that he is needed at home and can do nothing about it. The only thing that drives me from Ruth and the children is the deep awareness that it is God's will for me, and that it is for the salvation and blessing of many lives in deep need. I am everlastingly grateful to the Lord for a faithful wife who is willing to pay any price in order that the work of God be carried through to victory.

I was holding meetings in a Women's Auxiliary Corps (WAC) camp near Chattanooga when word came that my frail little Ruth Ellyn had double pneumonia and was hanging between life and death. My first impulse was to throw a few things into a briefcase and take the next train home. Before I could do that, the "Chief," Al Kunz, put his strong arm around my shoulders as I stood silently weeping. "Phil," he said, his voice full of compassion, "you had better pray about this before you make a move."

This was good advice. As I knelt before the Lord, I felt the calm assurance that if I would stay where I was, preaching the good news so needed by these women, God would take care of my little one in the hospital back in New Jersey. I talked to Ruth by telephone, and felt the rocklike strength of her trust in our Lord, and her readiness for whatever might come. Then I told her that hundreds of these needy girls were coming to Christ, and that others, disoriented, far from their homes, were being helped.

We both knew that I had made the right decision—to stay. I have seen a number of men limited or ruined in their ministry by a wife who begged her husband to turn aside from the Lord's will; but Ruth has never said anything to hinder my obedience to God. On the contrary, she has always hidden her tears and heartaches, so that they would not add to my burden.

The Lord's answers to prayer during those war years were often miraculous, even in such a matter as catching a train when it looked impossible. One day Conrad Baehr, a fellow team member, had to catch a local train in order to make connections with an express for New York and his next PTL assignment. If he missed it, important work would suffer. It was my job to get him to the station in Evansville, Indiana, but we didn't start on time—and we had a flat tire! The crossing gates at the station were going up as we arrived, and the back of the train was slowly passing. It was all my fault.

"Connie," I said, "do you believe that God can stop that train for us?"

"Yes," he replied, "but we just failed to get here on time. It was our mistake."

I felt the discouragement in his voice. "Well," I declared, "if the Lord didn't make up for our mistakes we would never get anything done. Let's ask Him!"

We crossed the tracks, drove one block, and swung left. I

could see the smoke puffing up between old warehouses. At the
next corner, I swung left again. Driving as fast as I dared, I
turned right to chase the train along a bumpy, cobblestone street.
The conductor was standing on the rear platform, calmly punching tickets and stuffing them into his pockets. As we drew along-
side, I yelled, "Hey, is this train going to stop before leaving
town?"

He shrugged indifferently, scarcely looking up. For a dozen
blocks we kept abreast of the rear car; then, just as it reached a
point where the street petered out into an overgrown field and
the rails curved off to the north, the train stopped. Just for a moment!

Connie jumped out with a suitcase, and gave one great leap,
landing almost on top of the startled conductor. I threw up two
more suitcases, but one was not Connie's, and he threw it back.
As the train moved around the bend, Connie's tall figure could be
seen on the back platform, a wide smile on his handsome face as
he waved his gray homburg.

On another day, the slow milk train I was riding up from Jackson, Mississippi, arrived at Memphis an hour late. I had barely ten
minutes to cross to the other railroad station and catch the crack
streamliner, "Tennessean." Praying as I ran, I dived into a phone
booth and called the stationmaster.

"Hold the 'Tennessean,' I'll be right over," I told him authori-
tatively.

"Who is it? Who is it?" he asked as I hung up the receiver.

Several minutes later, I came hurrying through the gate followed by an overloaded, sweating porter. The trainmen were
standing there with their watches in their hands. "Okay, men," I
said; "let's go!"

Whatever they replied was lost on me. I was already aboard
and we were rolling out of the station. Finally the conductor
came through, punching tickets. When I showed him my sleeper
reservation he pushed his cap back on his head. "There isn't even
a *car* on the train with this number," he muttered.

"Well," I laughed, "I'll just sit here."

He looked at me. "I'm sorry, but these seats are all reserved."

"Then I'll stand in a corner."

I was so happy to be on board and homeward bound after a long absence that sitting or standing was all the same. But I *was* tired, and it must have showed. At any rate, a woman who had been within earshot got up and went back through the train to consult her husband who was riding in a day coach on his soldier's pass. On returning, she asked me, "Would you be interested in an upper berth?"

My answer was prompt and delighted. She explained that their little boy always got sick on the train sitting up, so she had bought the upper berth as well as the lower one in order to have use of the two seats by day. "My little boy can sleep with me in the lower," she said.

When, later on, I told the story to some church ladies, one or two of them were shocked at my temerity in delaying a train. I pointed out to them that preaching the gospel is more important than any other business in the world, and that, while personally I am nothing, carrying out His Great Commission has top priority.

"If the Lord were displeased with what I did," I reasoned, "how do you explain His provision of an upper berth for me?"

When our son David was born, I was back in itinerant chalk-talk church evangelism, and two hundred miles from the hospital. As Ruth was being wheeled from the delivery room, weak as she was, she stopped her rolling bed to call me from a telephone in the corridor.

"You're the father of a husky boy with red-gold fuzz on his little round head," she informed me. I couldn't mistake the happiness in her voice.

Three years passed, and again I waited at home the allotted two weeks. Then I had to leave for a children's camp, back in the wild mountains of western Virginia. I was finishing a Bible message to a hundred camp children when a girl counselor beckoned to me from the doorway. With her lips she silently shaped the word, "Telephone!"

The instrument was at the end of a long, overworked party line, where, with each receiver lifted by a curious neighbor, the voice becomes weaker. Twenty people must have been listening in. I could barely hear the voice of a dear friend at the other end.

"What is it?" I shouted, hoarse with anxiety.

After a few blurred repetitions, the reply came through faintly but distinctly: "Twin boys!"

For some months I had been joking about becoming the father of twins. The sudden reality of it nearly floored me.

But I am getting ahead of my story. Not long after the end of the war I was on a platform with Glenn Wagner, one of the best speakers and organizers of the Pocket Testament League. Glenn was telling how desperately the people of conquered Japan needed the Word of God. General MacArthur, he said, had opened the door wide to the gospel, calling for a thousand missionaries, and the Japanese response was already assured. Men, women, boys, and girls would come running from all directions when a little Gospel of John was offered, and joyfully accept the gift. The General had asked Glenn Wagner to launch a huge distribution campaign.

I was deeply impressed, and after the meeting I asked Glenn if he thought I might be of service in Japan. He did, and almost before I realized it, God had raised up the financial support I would need.

5.

Incredible Japan

The airport in Seattle, Washington, was practically deserted when, in the middle of the night, I prepared to embark on the long flight to Japan by way of Alaska. At the desk, I was disconcerted to learn that ten pounds of overweight would cost me far more dollars than I had to spare.

"I'm sorry," I told the man behind the desk, "I can't pay overweight. I'm a missionary, on a tight budget."

I was going to add that I would have to leave something behind when the man suggested, "Why don't you put some of the heavy items in your pockets?"

Hurriedly I rummaged through my duffel and transferred to my person an electric shaver, several books, an extra pair of shoes, and other things until I bulged like the stuffed cheeks of a pocket gopher. The man looked at the arrow on the scales. "Now you're underweight," he said. "Put something back."

I put back everything that I had taken out, one thing at a time —and the weight was *just right!* We were both pleased about it, though I was still mystified by the whole thing as I boarded the plane. A Philippine diplomat and I were the only passengers, and most of the plane's interior was filled with huge crates of military supplies.

By morning we were droning along steadily above and to the west of the spectacular Canadian Rockies. How anyone can look upon such breathtaking beauty and say there is no God is beyond my understanding! Their vast mountain ranges were blanketed in snow; and, thrusting through that shimmering cover, their dark, jagged peaks notched the landscape as far as I could see. This was the first segment of a tremendous panorama, unfolding over western Alaska, down the east coast of Siberia and on to Japan.

War-ravaged Japan! The chaotic ruin of its great economy shocked me beyond telling; and Hiroshima was worse. One day I heard the story of a man who survived that first atomic holocaust.

Toward the end of World War II, a Japanese Christian who fearlessly preached the gospel in the streets was living on the main island of Honshu. He was a dentist by profession, but his love for Christ and his fellowmen made telling the Good News his first business. Those were the days when Japanese warlords were fiercely promoting the doctrine of their emperor's divinity, knowing it to be of major importance to the nation's last-ditch effort. Though their dream of world conquest was fast fading, absolute faith in an emperor-god could still unite their people. Every Nipponese flier who crashed his bomb-loaded *kamikaze* plane into an enemy battleship would go straight to heaven, they affirmed.

One day the secret police heard the dentist-evangelist declare that Christ, the Only Begotten Son of God, was going to return to the world as King of Kings. Immediately they arrested him. In court, the judge asked grimly, "You say that Jesus Christ is coming back to this earth to rule? At that time, will the emperor bow before him, or will he bow before the emperor?"

A deathly silence fell upon the courtroom. With every eye fixed upon him, the "criminal" replied, "When Christ returns, *every* knee shall bow to Him—including the emperor's."

"Treason!" shouted the judge. After sentencing the preacher to death, he ordered him sent to Hiroshima for execution. Such a "traitor" was not considered worthy of a common prison cell; so the soldiers dug a hole *under* the prison, and the dentist was flung into it. Scraps of food were thrown down to him, as if he were an animal; and no sanitary arrangements were provided.

One day an American bomber appeared over Hiroshima. Sirens wailed. The inhabitants scrambled for their air-raid shelters. Most of them were military personnel, since women and children had already been evacuated. They waited in the shelters for the shock of bombs, but, mysteriously, none came. The plane disappeared in the distance, and sirens sounded the "all clear." The people came out to see only a large parachute slowly descending over the city.

As they watched, the sky exploded with a brilliance fiercer than the sun's. Eighty-thousand souls were incinerated or fatally burned. As in the dreadful, prophetic picture in Zechariah 14:12, "their flesh was consumed while they stood upon their feet." In that blast, Hiroshima ceased to be.

But the despised little dentist, safely hidden in his hole under the prison floor, was untouched. He lived to continue preaching the gospel of Christ, the King of Kings.

"Surely the wrath of man shall praise Thee; and the remainder of wrath shalt Thou restrain" (Psa. 76:10).

When I saw Hiroshima's frightful ruins, a scanty populace was living in shacks made of tin and broken pieces of wood or bamboo. Of all the large buildings, only parts of two were standing— gaunt walls of heavy reinforced concrete. On one wall I saw the faint shadow of a human form that had been vaporized by atomic heat. I met the "number one atomic bomb victim," whose back and arms bore heavy scar tissue, like knotted ropes. He had been converted to Christ since the blast.

While actual destruction had been confined to the great cities, we saw on every side the cruel impoverishment of a once-thriving nation. Overpopulation added heavily to its burdens. Only the

Japanese capacity for hard work and intelligent application to knotty problems gave an inkling of its future "resurrection" to a splendid prosperity.

At that time, the feudal community system, together with poverty, bound rural folk to their own locality. For most Japanese, free travel was next to impossible; and this was especially true during the war years. At one large prison we were given a new sidelight on "incredible" Japan. We were told that when American bombing reached that area, the prison officials sent all of the prisoners home. "When the attacks are over we will notify you to return," they were informed. And upon being notified, all of the inmates did come back. So few people moved from one part of the interior to another that tracing prisoners was no problem.

Some of the "strange" behavior that we noticed was simply an answer to necessity. We watched farmers building heavy stone walls out into an area devastated by mountain torrents; they were reclaiming precious land for growing crops from rocky stream beds. Others were building aqueducts, miles long, to water little terraced fields through sluice gates. These fields, curving with the mountainside, were sometimes a hundred yards long, and a yard or two wide.

In one meeting on the island of Shikoku, the pastor of the church went to sleep during my preaching. I was offended and upset. I even slipped into my message a remark critical of those who failed to pay attention to God's Word. Later I was to recall my remark with burning shame, hoping that Mabel Francis,* my interpreter, somehow deflected my thrust at the sensitive Japanese audience. After the service, she gently reminded me that this pastor, with other evangelical leaders, had through the war years worn himself out ministering to his bewildered, desperate flock.

* Veteran pioneer missionary of the Christian and Missionary Alliance, now over ninety years old.

He had known semistarvation besides, and all this explained why he fell asleep in the church. I felt low enough to crawl under a rug!

I was slated to be in Japan for three-and-a-half months, but I had been there only a short time when I knew the Lord wanted me to return for a second stretch of at least six months. I wavered, recalling Ruth's face wet with tears as she and our three little ones watched my plane taxi away at the New York International Airport. And there was the letter that a fellow missionary had carried about in his pocket for a month before delivering it to me—a letter from Ruth, telling of her injury in a traffic accident.

Ruth was coming home from a meeting with two other mothers, in Greensboro, North Carolina, when a young marine on leave drove through a red light and smashed into their car. Ruth, who had been sitting in the middle of the front seat, was hurled into the street. An ambulance took the three women to the hospital, and for hours Ruth remained unconscious, with a brain concussion. Finally, through the murky fog that seemed to envelop her senses, she heard the faraway voice of the doctor saying, "Now, if you can tell us the whereabouts of your husband, we will notify him to come at once."

Ruth struggled for speech. It came: "My husband . . . is . . . in Japan."

The doctor's voice responded, "Then we will send him a cablegram at once."

"No," the words came slowly from the bed, "no telegram! When I am . . . better . . . I will write him a letter. I don't want . . . anything . . . to hinder his work for the Lord."

Could I take another separation, for six months? Could Ruth? But the more I moved about Japan, the more I felt the acute hunger of a people, for spiritual truth—hunger that only the gospel could satisfy. I knew Ruth and I must find strength to carry on for Him Who said, "My grace is sufficient for thee."

It seemed as if I had barely returned home, when I was off again on my second tour of duty in Japan. This time I went by Hawaii. After long, droning hours over the Pacific's endless expanse, our potbellied, double-decked prop-plane came in for a landing at tiny Wake Island just before dawn. There were a few low military buildings at the edge of the long runway, and the black hulk of a sunken Japanese ship looming in the darkness along the barren coast, but I sensed that there would be a spectacular sunrise.

I started down the ramp with my movie camera. Some grease monkeys were taking the cowling off a motor. I asked them, "How long will it take you to finish the job?"

"Oh, three or four hours," one man replied.

That, I thought, should give me plenty of time to take some excellent footage of a Pacific sunrise over famous Wake Island. I hurried away, watching for some tree or rock formation that could provide a striking silhouette against the brilliance that I knew would appear. I waited until the colors were very bright. Absorbed in my work, I forgot about time; and at last, still thinking of the beauty I'd filmed, I started back to the airport. I hadn't quite reached it when I saw the huge tail of my plane moving off down the runway behind the low buildings!

Horrified, I made for the radio tower at full gallop, took the stairs three at a time, and burst into the control room, shouting, "Hey! I'm supposed to be on that plane!"

The technicians turned to stare. Then one of them cut in the radio to intercept the lumbering behemoth. Somebody else said, "Come on, let's go!" and disappeared down the stairs. I followed, praying that I wouldn't be stranded for a week on that desolate speck of land. We piled into a pickup truck and shot down the runway like a flea chasing an elephant. Just as the plane turned for its takeoff at the far end of the runway, we overtook it; and moments later, through a small hatch in the monster's belly, I climbed safely aboard.

Once more, with time to think about the long six months that I'd have to be away from my young wife and my precious little ones, I prayed for courage.

Back on the job, that prayer was answered, often in unexpected ways. One day, during my second tour of duty, a charming American couple invited me to share a Japanese meal. We were practically strangers, but during the delightful repast our acquaintance ripened quickly. My hostess told me how she had accepted Christ in Westwood, New Jersey, at the close of a Sunday school rally day service, at the age of nine, when a young chalk artist made the gospel clear with quick sketches—mine!

"But that isn't all," her husband told me. "When you came back to the states from your first tour of duty in Japan, God challenged us through you to come here to Tokyo, to serve the Lord."

"And here we are," my hostess said with a happy smile, "working with Japanese students."

As I got up to leave, I hardly noticed that my legs were pins and needles from sitting cross-legged so long.

For over a month, Russ Meade, talented accordionist, Nambu San, our interpreter, and I lived on a shoestring. We were almost entirely out of funds, but we started out from Tokyo trusting the Lord to keep us going. Just before we left, an American businessman bought us a big box full of jars of jelly and peanut butter. Responding to General MacArthur's plea, he had come to Japan to distribute tracts on the street and to do whatever else he could for the Lord. His gift box, together with bread and a watery bottled drink, made up our three meals a day.

Unable to afford hotels, we drove out of town and slept in the truck beside some country road. Usually when we made arrangements for a meeting with dignified city officials, they would ask where we would be staying, so that they might contact us if necessary. With typical Japanese finesse, Nambu San, my gifted interpreter, always replied, "It is not certain where we will be staying." What he actually meant was, "We don't know along what mountain stream we will park our truck tonight."

On one trip, Russ Meade, Nambu San, and I took a narrow gravel road that wound back from the west coast to a mountain-rimmed town. Roads like this were in a bad state of disrepair, since all of Japan's manpower, and even boy power, had been thrown into the war effort. After bouncing along for hours, we were brought to a full stop. A landslide had sliced our road clean away, leaving nothing but a smooth clay chute down to a raging torrent.

Night came on before we found another road leading to the same town. We parked on a triangular bit of land which jutted out from the road above a fifty-foot precipice, and crawled into our bunks.

In the first gray light of morning, I clambered out to take the first shift at the wheel, and Nambu chose a position where he could direct me back onto the road. I was still half-asleep. With the motor turning over, I shifted into reverse, so as to turn the truck around. Suddenly Nambu began waving his arms wildly and shouting in Japanese—and I felt the back of the truck begin to sag on the cliffside! I did the fastest gear shift of my life, and just barely pulled back to safety. If we had gone over the cliff, the Japanese would have respectfully buried our bodies, but resurrected our smashed vehicle.

After distributing large quantities of scripture portions in the mountain town, we returned to the west coast of the island and traveled from one fishing village to another, setting up meetings.

Russ Meade played the accordion; I drew gospel scenes in chalk and preached. Nambu San interpreted for us with skill and wonderful patience. He had left his law studies at the university to help us, though his family had strongly opposed this move. Nambu felt that our Pocket Testament League effort was of greatest importance to his people, and he knew that he might never again have such a wonderful chance to serve Christ and them.

Preaching by interpretation had obvious drawbacks. For one thing, it was hard for the preacher to know how his hearers were responding. And I found I had to avoid confusing idioms, like "tickled to death." When one evangelist used that phrase, his interpreter bravely declared that the man in question "scratched himself until he died!"

I usually started my messages with a chalk drawing of beautiful Japan, then told how God in the beginning created the heavens and the earth. I went on to explain how man rebelled against his creator, bringing sin and suffering upon the whole human race. I pointed out the need of every man to obtain forgiveness through Christ. Using Romans 3:22–23, I drew a quick sketch of a rich man and a poor beggar, and, showing in the space between them a heart covered with stains, I illustrated the condition of every person apart from the free gift of God. While Russ Meade's accordion provided background music, I drew the Cross of Calvary and introduced God's offer of salvation.

In every town where we stopped, a milling crowd fought to get the small Gospels of John that we gave out, and as we drove on we could see the people reading them intently, with inscrutable faces. More than ninety-five percent of Japanese are literate, and they truly prized our little gifts. Included in each one was our offer to mail a New Testament to anyone who wrote in to Tokyo after finishing the Gospel.

God knows how many souls were born anew through reading

these portions of His Word. I know of a Japanese shopkeeper who received a Testament directly from a missionary. He bowed low with typical Japanese courtesy, lifting the little book with both hands to his forehead, formally expressing his thanks to the giver. The missionary drove on. The shopkeeper took his Testament home and began to read it daily, with great care. Struck by its vital message, he soon was rising an hour earlier in the morning and closing his shop an hour sooner in the evening, to study it. He gathered several philosopher friends in his home so that they all could study this amazing Book together. As they probed deeper and deeper into the Gospels and Epistles, they realized that there were other holy scriptures which belonged with these. When the missionary came again to their town they looked him up, to ask how they might obtain the rest of the Book—the Old Testament.

You can imagine that missionary's joy at hearing how through one New Testament these Japanese scholars had found Christ, and how the leader had become a "missionary" and instructor, even painting diagrammatic charts to clarify such great teachings as our Lord's return.

Once, far back in the interior, Russ Meade, Nambu San, and I drove into a fairyland valley where no trace of today's onrushing civilization could be seen. Gaunt power poles, glaring billboards, and sky-smirching factory chimneys could have been half a world away, and even the sound of our motor seemed to desecrate that lovely place. Cherry trees in full bloom closed in about us, their double-petaled pink blossoms glorious in the sunlight, and in the distance rose a gigantic backdrop of snow-clad mountain peaks. Neat little fields formed a charming geometric pattern. They spoke of much toil and a love of orderly beauty. So did the houses, all built in the traditional Japanese style. The whole picture was too perfect to seem real.

We stopped at a quaint old country house where we were to

pass the night. We admired its curved wooden gables, its tiled roof, and its sliding doors. The patron and his wife had come out on the porch to greet us, but instead of bowing at the waist, they got down on their knees and bowed until their foreheads touched the polished floor. I whispered to Nambu San, "What do we do now?"

"We do the same," he replied. So down we went. The couple, pleased by my response, continued to bow up and down in polite acknowledgment. After several minutes of this, Nambu whispered, "It is enough. Too much courtesy hard on the back." And we all rose to our feet.

I recall a meeting in another interior town, chiefly because of a young man we met there. What marked him out from the rest, sitting cross-legged on the floor of the large school auditorium, was his full, bushy beard. Beards like that were not common in Japan, so I thought he must be a monk from some Shintoist monastery. His eyes and every line of his body showed intense interest as he watched the drawings and listened to the sermon. He remained after the service with many others, who thus signified their desire to accept Christ and to receive counseling. When we were ready to take down my easel and pack up, the bearded young man was still there.

"Nambu," I suggested, "talk with that man a bit and find out who he is."

Nambu San talked with him a good while, and I could see their earnestness. Afterward, Nambu told me that our young friend was not a monk, but an artist. His father had died. This left his elder brother, according to Japanese tradition, both titular and absolute head of the family. Now the young man's longing to follow an art career was frustrated, because his overbearing, materialistic brother was forcing him to work in the fields at common labor.

The young artist had come to town that afternoon, feeling sadder and more depressed than usual, and hearing our truck's loudspeaker announce the meeting, he had said to himself, "Perhaps this is what I need!"

After the meeting, at about midnight, we were driving slowly through one of the dark, narrow, cobblestone streets that led out into the country. Our headlights picked out the shadowy figure of a man who stepped out of our way to flatten himself against a wall. It was our bearded artist.

I said, "Stop the car, Russ. Let's give him a lift."

The young man's acceptance was deeply courteous. He had been heading back to the family farm on the mountainside. He climbed into the cab and sat a little forward, looking straight ahead as we started up. Clearly it was his first ride in a motor vehicle, but as Nambu talked with him he relaxed. He told Nambu that Jesus now lived in his heart, so that he could go back and submit himself to his brother without bitterness.

With this joyful news, we burst into song, using the few Japanese choruses we knew by heart. When we came to a narrow path that crossed our road, he got out, spoke briefly to Nambu, bowed low, and was soon lost in the darkness.

"His parting words to me," said Nambu San, "were, 'Now the darkness is no longer depressing, for I have the light of Christ within!' "

On another occasion we were traveling with Mabel Francis, one of the most radiant saints of God I have ever known. She was at that time seventy-six years of age, and still riding her bicycle over all kinds of roads on the Master's business. Hers was the power of a Christ-filled life; and how she loved the Japanese people! Just knowing her changed so many lives, including mine!

After a meeting that we held on the island of Shikoku, I saw Mabel kneeling, Japanese-fashion, on the floor of the auditorium, talking with a round-faced peasant woman who was weeping unrestrainedly. Such emotion is seldom seen in Japan, since to reveal one's feelings is considered bad taste. Later Mabel told us why the floodgates of this woman's heart had broken. She had received Christ. She knew that her terrible sin was now forgiven, and she had peace in her Savior, but her tears overflowed.

The woman's story was rooted in a basic problem of Japan— overpopulation, together with the poverty it causes. Whatever interrupts communal farm work is frowned upon, but this poor housewife, who must leave her young family in the care of an old crone and work from dawn till dark in the fields, had gotten pregnant again. When the village fathers learned of it, they ordered her to get rid of the child, so that her toil should not be hindered. With greatest reluctance she submitted to a primitive method of abortion known to the desperately poor. And then, as she saw the little dead body, the fruit of her womb, a feeling of terrible guilt overwhelmed her. It possessed her until she fled to the compassionate arms of Jesus, Who had died for her sin and the sins of all. I cannot doubt that, through our ministry, night after night, the Savior met the needs of many other people, binding up their broken hearts, drying the scalding tears.

Kin Ichiro Endo, a Christian businessman who became one of my dearest friends, was financially wiped out during the war. His large printing establishment was destroyed in an incendiary bombing raid, and when the war ended his workers were either scattered or dead. He had no capital with which to start over again; yet God helped him to do it, and when the Pocket Testament League arrived, Kin was ready to print the sixteen million Gospels that we needed. I asked him how it happened. He said, "Prayer is my breathing."

Then he continued, softly smiling, "I was riding on train when United States army officer came into diner and sat down opposite me. North American wanted fried eggs, sun side up; waiter not understand, even though I explain officer's request. So I went back to kitchen and cooked eggs myself. Colonel was delighted. During conversation he learned I experienced printer in Tokyo. He contracted me to print materials needed by occupation forces, and supplied the presses."

Kin Ichiro not only handled our PTL printing, but he went on many trips with our teams, as interpreter.

Another capable interpreter was Sato San. At first acquaintance I looked askance at him, because he belonged to a Pentecostal group. I was sure that behind his smiling countenance lurked some offbeat and therefore dangerous doctrinal beliefs. However, during all our association I never heard him promote special doctrines. Wherever we went he manifested his closeness to God. There were moments when, even sitting at the table, he seemed to be in another world, with his Bible in his lap, his eyes closed, and his lips moving in prayer. My feelings about Sato San soon changed. I was at first apprehensive, then amused by his "quaint" ways; but then something happened which gave me a glimpse of Sato's true inner life.

One day I was sent with a panel truck to move Sato's family and belongings from where he was then living to a little room that he had finally found for them. I knew only that he had a wife and four small children. There was a dreary drizzle of rain, unpleasant, I thought, for moving personal belongings. After a twenty-minute drive through downtown Tokyo, we pulled up at a bombed-out church, of which nothing was left but the foundations and the concrete floor. It was a pathetic reminder of the last century's inflexible missionary methods—just the rubble of a once beautiful, imposing, expensive *Gothic* structure. And this was where Sato San's family had been living—not in a basement but in a dirt-walled cave dug under the foundations!

I stooped low, sliding in the mud of the entrance tunnel to enter a tiny square room. Here were a small, low Japanese table with a crack down the middle, a rickety old chest of drawers, a primitive charcoal stove, and a crude rack for clothes. Sato's four little children were playing happily in the damp semigloom. But in contrast to these dungeonlike surroundings, the very Spirit of Victory was shining in the faces of Sato San and his little wife.

We carried out their few belongings and set them, half an hour later, in the one room which would now house the six of them. As Sato San and I returned to the PTL compound, I reflected that he, knowing both English and Japanese, could be enjoying a good position with the occupation forces and a substantial income; yet he and his family were enduring hardships and long separations for the cause of Christ.

Sato San's Pentecostal ties, which I considered outside the pale of wholesome doctrine, didn't seem to be doing him any harm. On the contrary, he appeared to be living closer to our Lord than I, with my smug pride in scriptural correctness. I was learning that I couldn't label each Christian sect either "all good" or "all bad." Step by step the Lord was leading me, an impulsive, prejudiced preacher, to higher levels of Christian love and understanding. I was coming to value very highly the Japanese evangelicals with whom I worked. Their spirit of sacrifice, their courtesy and endless patience with our blundering self-sufficiency, impressed me, and their kindness enriched my soul.

Looking back, I know that I was leaning too heavily on advertising, on chalk pictures and music, and too lightly on God's Holy Spirit. Yet the Lord did bless us with wonderful responses to His Word, printed, preached, and pictured. We prized especially our opportunities to visit prisons. The inmates were always eager to help us carry in huge quantities of Japanese Gospels of John, along with our bulky projector, screen-sound equipment, and easel. They watched with rapt attention our showing of such Moody films as *God of Creation*, and the chalk drawings. After each prison visit, requests poured in to the PTL office in Tokyo, saying, "I have read and reread the little book and deeply desire to receive a New Testament."

There were many times when we Americans must have cut a ridiculous figure in Japanese eyes. One such occasion stands out vividly. We had loaded the truck on a flatcar bound for Tokyo, and Nambu San had offered to stay with the truck, to watch over our precious equipment on the four-day trip. This left me alone on a passenger train with two or three phrases that I had memorized in pidgin Japanese. The train was stopped in a huge railroad station one morning at daybreak, and I was calmly shaving in the washroom, when there came a knock on the door. I opened it, to face an excited porter. "Changee tlain!" he exclaimed.

I smiled and made signs that I would be done shaving in a minute or two; but that was the wrong response.

"Changee tlain! Changee tlain!" he shouted, with a wild look in his eye.

I caught on. Clad only in pants and undershirt, face lathered, shaving brush in one hand and razor in the other, I marched down the whole length of the platform, past hundreds of observant Japanese, with the little porter carrying my suitcase, shirt, tie, and other belongings ahead of me. Not one audible snicker followed me, but I know that in America my predicament would have drawn more hoots, whistles, and catcalls than a cageful of monkeys.

In Tokyo and in other large cities we held some tremendous rallies. Gil Dodds, the world champion miler, came over to help us. Wherever we went, he ran against the best Japanese runners. I remember standing beside him one time when he was putting on his spiked shoes. We were watching the Japanese athletes warm up.

"Those boys are sure in top shape," Gil said, admiringly. "Just look at them run!"

Then he shook his head, muttering something about not having had time to keep in condition because of constant traveling to so many meetings. The way he talked, I wondered if he were going to lose the race. I even thought of sneaking off somewhere, so that when he did lose I wouldn't be caught in the backwash of embarrassment.

Sure enough, when the starter's gun cracked, those fifteen Japanese were off like the wind, leaving old Gil to jog along behind as if he'd already given up hope. My heart was in my throat! But then Gil began gradually to overtake the Japanese runners. Before long he was among them, and at the last half of the last lap he was far out in front, his smooth, long strides around the turn making it seem almost easy. One beautifully muscled national nearly killed himself trying to cut Gil's lead, but it was no use. It was always like that. Gil finished away out ahead of the nearest competition.

At the close of each event he would come to the rally platform, still breathing hard, and give his personal testimony to Christ's saving power. Fukuda San was his eloquent interpreter. At the largest of all track meets, held in Tokyo, the North American announcer took the microphone with the apparent intention of heading off Gil's personal witness for Christ, but Gil wasn't there just to win laurels. He was out to win souls for the Captain of his Salvation; so he forcibly took the mike from that smart North American, and told the crowd that the greatest thrill of his life was not when he broke the world's record for the indoor mile at Madison Square Garden. It was when he received Jesus Christ as his personal Savior.

Only eternity will show how many of the sports-loving, hero-worshiping Japanese were brought to Christ at that great rally.

For several days before our stadium meeting in Yokahama, PTL trucks went through the streets with their loudspeakers announcing the program which would feature Gil Dodds, Glenn

Wagner, and my chalk drawings. The city was plastered with Oriental-style posters showing those of us who would participate.

As in Tokyo, a sea of humanity surged toward the great indoor stadium on the meeting day. After taking off their *gaita* at the door, they poured in and sat on the floor. We had roped off the part of the stands that was behind the platform, since my pictures, drawn on an enormous easel, could not be seen from that direction. However, when the front part of the stadium was filled, the human tide spilled over the ropes and crowded the entire section right up to the roof.

All went well until I started to draw. Then the two or three thousand people who could not see the drawing on the easel got to their feet and began pushing down to the main floor. For a while the bedlam of shouting and pushing looked like a riot. The frantic policemen were tossed about like a few chips on a flash flood. Fortunately there were no chairs. In the end, those on the floor—men, women, and children—were crowded together like sardines in a can. The shoving and shouting gradually subsided, and in a short while we were able to continue.

Before the end of my tour of duty in Japan, I contracted a racking cough. I was in a run-down condition before that, eating the meager rations that were available to us after the war, holding meetings until we lost count of them, and traveling constantly without rest. But sick or well, there was no stopping. In most of the interior towns and cities where we brought God's Word there were then no missionaries and few Christians. Many Japanese, weakened by war conditions, were dying. Old people, at the end of their strength, sometimes dropped in the street, and in the hospitals workers made daily rounds through the wards, removing the dead. Often there were two or three debilitated patients in one bed. So many dying, without Christ! I couldn't quit!

Burning with fever, I lay in a bunk in the rear of the truck while Russ drove. When we reached the town where a meeting was to be held, they put me to bed on the floor, Japanese-style, with quilts laid on the *tatami,* woven straw mats. Russ and Nambu then obtained official permission to hold the meeting. Afterward, they toured the streets with the truck's loudspeaker announcing our program. Later, at the meeting place, they set up my easel and the public-address system. At the last minute I went to the cold, drafty building to draw and preach.

The cough nearly doubled me over at times, but God gave strength to get through the meetings in several towns. I would have gone to a doctor, but there was none to be had.

One day as I lay on the floor of my room in a mountain town, very weak and utterly miserable, I sensed that several persons had come in and were talking about me. Then someone kneeling behind me laid cool, firm hands on my hot forehead. I looked up to see that they belonged to a round-faced, weather-beaten peasant woman. Her head was raised, and her eyes, behind small, steel-rimmed spectacles, were tightly closed. Her lips moved as she spoke softly to our Heavenly Father in Japanese. I recognized His Name, and I knew that she must be asking Him to make me well.

This was the first time that anybody had prayed for me with the laying on of hands. I had been taught that it was not necessary to "lay hands on the sick" today or to "anoint with oil," and that it was proper to bow the head instead of raising the face toward heaven; but this old Japanese lady was praying for me compassionately, in the Name of Jesus, and God was very near to both of us.

She finished her prayer and left the room, gently sliding the bamboo and paper panels shut behind her. That night I slept like a baby. When I awoke in the morning, the fever and its cause—pneumonia or whatever—were gone. I had been healed, and I knew that I would be able to return to the states to take my next assignment in the islands of the Caribbean.

6.

Latin America Calling

I found the Windward Islands more spectacular than anything I had imagined. Here was everything to catch an artist's eye: tall palms above dazzling white beaches; proud sails gliding among the gray banana boats with their red- or blue-banded stacks; and, in forest glades, the flash of brilliant bird plumage.

The people were as warm and friendly as their land—folk who laughed much in spite of prevalent sickness and grinding poverty. Innumerable monkeys and other furry pets were everywhere, as were the "buzzards," or turkey vultures—street cleaners, protected by law.

I was teamed with Dit Fenton (at present director of the Latin American missions), Sterling Krause, our song leader, and his wife Evangeline, from Minnesota. All of them were wonderful company. Dit was our setup man and emcee while Evangeline played the vibraharp and sang lovely duets with her husband.

In one of the larger cities on Trinidad Island we had a roofed platform set up between the barnlike church and the rambling school complex. It was a nearly ideal site to handle the swarming crowds that turned out each night. They numbered between one and two thousand people, mostly black, with a good number of Hindus and a sprinkling of whites. And how they loved to sing, quickly learning the gospel choruses that Sterling taught them. They heartily enjoyed the chalk drawings, and several hundred responded to the clear-cut gospel preaching by making a public profession of faith in the Savior during that campaign.

On my second trip to the Islands, Bill Thompson, also of the Latin American missions, served as team coordinator. Bill would have drawn attention in any crowd, with his erect figure, his shock of graying hair, and his air of distinction. His vivacious wife Pearl was our pianist.

Very much against my wife's advice, my youngest brother, Benny, came with us. There was no question about Ben's soul-winning zeal or the outgoing friendliness which animated his six-foot-three frame; but his folksy, "immature" performance as a song leader had not been well received by our congregation back in the states. Some of the church people had persuaded Ruth that Benny would be a hindrance on our mission tour—"Too crude, too green," and so forth.

My insistence on taking him, and Ruth's insistence that I ought not to, caused one of the very few sharp quarrels that Ruth and I have had in our married life. I blew up, stormed out of the house, jumped into the car, and drove around until I had cooled off. Then I confessed that I'd been wrong to lose my temper, but I didn't change my mind or my determination to take Ben. I felt that the half-dozen chords that he could find on his guitar would be enough to accompany the simple duets we would sing, and I knew that the simple island people would love Ben's bighearted sincerity.

That is how it turned out. But I left the states with a different anxiety nagging my thoughts. It seemed that almost every time I went overseas, something happened to Ruth!

This time, just before I started out, she fell and banged her foot. The swelling that followed was bad enough to send her to the doctor. X rays showed that cancer had attacked the bone on the outside of her foot, leaving only a shell, and that shell had collapsed. The surgeon grafted in a piece of bone from her pelvis. In answer to prayer, God prevented a recurrence of the cancer but Ruth was on crutches, her leg in a cast, taking care of our small, energetic twin boys, who often ran in opposite directions.

I carried the haunting recollection of the day when those three-year-olds disappeared. We hunted high and low for them, calling frantically. They were not in the house. As we checked the yard, we heard little voices, and looked up to see Jimmy and Joey two stories above the ground, teetering on the edge of the neighbor's roof! Somebody had left a tall ladder leaning against the building.

Worry about their next escapade would be pointless. God had taken care of my precious family and would guard them in my absence. Once on our way, I drew strength from Ben's deep prayer-life, and thrilled to his untiring, person-to-person evangelism which brought home to me how much I lacked in that area.

In the Islands, we found that the people loved our catchy, ballad-style choruses and our duets accompanied by Ben's "four-chord" guitar. And at Kingston, Jamaica, Ben solved a problem that had the rest of us stumped. Inside the cathedrallike church building, packed with eighteen hundred people, the humid heat was oppressive, and there was no good place for my easel. There was no platform—only a pillbox pulpit at the top of a winding ladder—so we put the easel up in the choir loft. Those seated under the wide gallery could not see it at all.

After we'd held a few meetings in this building, Benny asked, "Why don't we go outside and hold meetings in the vacant lot across from here?"

The more I considered it, the more sense Benny's idea made. We had heard that in Jamaica, church custom forbade anybody entering the sanctuary without a jacket on. And a good many Islanders didn't own a jacket! Out-of-doors we could reach those, too, and in comfort.

The church committee was politely horrified by our suggestion. Preaching, they said, should be done in a sanctuary, and besides, in Jamaica one never knew when it might rain. Still, we insisted that we could do better outside, and we did. At our last two meetings in the vacant lot, attendance jumped to three thousand, with proportionately more people receiving Christ.

From then on, in the Caribbean area, we planned to have our first meeting in the local church, and after that as many meetings as possible in the open air. This method more than tripled the number of people who could get to hear us.

One Monday night, with no meeting scheduled, Benny and I went down to the poorest section of Kingston to hold an impromptu service. We went early, in order to look over the neighborhood. We saw that many of the shacks were made of tin from oil cans, wired or nailed to rough tree limbs or to old boards. Most of the dwellings were guarded by heavy, thorny hedges, each of which, rumor said, had a secret entrance, to discourage thieves.

We had come there unaware of any personal danger, and without telling our friends in the "respectable" part of town. Later on we were informed that even the police and the Salvation Army wisely left that area at nightfall.

With time to spare, Benny and I set up the easel in the yard of a small chapel, then drifted across the wide, sandy road to the large crowd which was watching a spiritist street meeting. It was typical of the weird "shows" which break out like a rash, night after night, all over that part of the world. Tom-toms were beating out a hypnotic rhythm; men chanted, women with eyes narrowed to slits swayed back and forth, all of them under the spell of drugs, evil spirits, or both.

Among the onlookers were a number of strangely garbed addicts who would be in high style at an anti-establishment riot or a "rock festival" today. The difference was that they carried machetes. They called themselves "Rastafaris," and belonged to a fa-

natical antiwhite movement related to the dreaded Mau Maus of
Africa. We had not yet learned about them, but Ben, who was
standing a few yards behind me, saw one of these characters point
to me and mutter, "Thar's some white mon. Le's kill 'm!"

Ben waded through the dark-skinned crowd to my side and
told me what he'd heard. Almost immediately we were surrounded by a dozen vicious types who glared at us with mari-
juana-spiked hatred and fingered their razor-edged weapons. A
machete, ordinarily used for cutting sugarcane, can behead an
enemy as neatly as an executioner's axe.

Ben had worked with stevedores on the waterfront, and had
been paymaster of a tough work gang on the Santa Fe Railroad;
but neither of us was trusting in "the arm of flesh." We were in
the midst of more than a hundred black people, now turning their
attention to us, with no hint of sympathy for our predicament.
But Ben and I were trusting God, and He gave us grace to be unafraid.

One small, wiry Rastafari began haranguing us about "tha
curse of tha white mon" and the supremacy of the black race. His
eyes were bloodshot, and he spat out his words with murderous
vehemence. He spoke excitedly in a strongly accented Afro-
English dialect. It was hard for us to follow what he was saying,
but we gathered that Ethiopia was the Promised Land, that Haile
Selassie (obviously without his consent) was their messiah, and
that the Rastafaris were destined to kill off the white oppressors,
leaving the world to black people.

The spokesman was working himself and his own little group
into an uncontrollable fury. The spiritist seance had stopped, and
the crowd was awaiting a bloody climax. I knew that I must cut
the murder harangue short—or die.

A day or two before, I had read a brief history of the Islands.
(How wonderfully God leads!) It told of dedicated British missionaries who went to prison and even to death to help the ances-

tors of these black people, because white slave owners had broken up black families, branded, tortured, and killed them as they pleased, and even set bear traps to catch runaways. The missionaries suffered with the slaves whose part they took, but their outcry reached all the way to Queen Victoria. She herself, a deeply earnest Christian, bought the slaves from their owners and set them free. The blacks had never forgotten it.

As all this flashed through my mind, I spoke up. "Look! I am interested in what you believe about Haile Selassie being King of Kings, and about Ethiopia. But *first,* I want you to know that we are *not* rich American tourists who have come here to live high and flaunt our money. We are Christian missionaries who have come to serve you people, by preaching the gospel."

A murmur of approval went through the crowd. All at once we were among friends. People pushed between us and the Rastafaris—people who would defend us now from all harm. This was the cue that I needed to invite everybody over to the churchyard to see pictures drawn in bright colors and to hear singing and guitar music. I promised to tell them about the *real* King of Kings.

They came, *en masse,* and among the thirty who stayed for counseling after the meeting were several of the bearded Rastafaris.

Even the rain, so unpredictable in the Islands, failed to spoil a single outdoor meeting for us in a whole month. Once, it began to pour in the middle of a service, just after I had finished a chalk drawing. The people scurried to shelter. Although the platform was protected by an overhanging roof, I assumed that the meeting was over, because getting chilled and wet makes the Islanders' dormant malaria flare up. But the church leaders pleaded with us not to leave; the crowd, they told us, would be back shortly.

Sure enough, within ten minutes the rain stopped, and the people flocked back to hear the preaching. This was clear evidence that they had not come just to be entertained with music and pictures. We had presented a crucified and risen Savior, and He was drawing them to Himself. "I, if I be lifted up from the earth, will draw all men unto me" (John 12:32).

We flew from island to island, and everywhere large crowds turned out to hear God's message. Three months of meetings brought a total attendance of 350,000, with about 3,000 professions of faith. Many of them were unforgettable. A beautiful Hindu girl was among those who turned to Christ in a certain coastal town. She told her white consort that she could no longer live with him as they had been doing. He did everything he could to change her mind, insisting that she could be "religious" and still be his mistress, but the girl knew better. She remained true to Christ, refusing to compromise.

While our first meeting in another town was getting under way, I saw the local rector glancing over the sermon notes which lay in my open Bible at his elbow. His face showed shocked disapproval. The notes that I had made for this first evangelistic message stated bluntly that one can be very sincere, can reform himself, can even be religious, and still not be saved. For salvation is transformation by Christ's power as He comes personally to live in our hearts. There is no other way.

In the early meetings of our campaign, this rector strongly opposed us, but as we continued with God's blessing, the very atmosphere of the community changed. So did the rector's attitude. As he saw some of the worst sinners in the area gloriously saved, made "new creatures in Christ," beyond all doubt, he was profoundly affected. On our closing night, this man, with deep emotion, publicly confessed to the great personal blessings he had received from God through our ministry.

Our Caribbean tour ended in British Guiana at a time of intense political unrest. Some individuals tried to convince the public that our coming was politically motivated. One candidate tried to keep people away from our meeting by holding a big political rally on the same night in the same town. However, God was with us, and the huge churchyard was packed, while the politico's rally amounted to nothing.

One religious leader publicly accused me of trickery. He said, "This man only pretends to draw his scenes. They are already formed on his easel. He causes them to appear simply by rubbing on the surface."

The next evening I invited anyone who wished to come to the platform and rub on the board to make a picture appear. Nobody moved. These people, most of them very poor in material things, were friendly to us, and responded warmly to our preaching of the "unsearchable riches of Christ."

While we were in British Guiana, an evangelical pastor who was a converted Hindu took me to see a heathen temple and witness one of its rites, brought over from India. The weather-stained temple was small and drab. As we watched, the priests prostrated themselves before a hideous, dirty idol that was visible in the shadowed interior. Then they came outside, and one began beating a sacred drum while the other chanted softly, with closed eyes. All at once the chanter began to shake, or rather to *be* shaken, like a rag doll. His head rolled loosely. His movements appeared to be quite involuntary, with his hands and arms dangling grotesquely. His bare feet rose and fell alternately, about six inches, slapping the ground.

We were told that though he seemed unconscious, he was communing with the spirit of the temple's god, and that this god would tell him where to locate a lost cow, or how to answer some worshiper's personal problem.

Finally the drummer stopped beating. He pressed sacred ashes on the chanter's forehead, and the man's shaking gradually ceased. Blank and watery eyes resumed their conscious look of unutterable despair. I can never forget them! I had the creepy feeling that I'd been in the presence of demons, and that I shouldn't have been there.

Later on, in Argentina, recalling this experience would help me to recognize demonic influence in religious behavior. By that time, however, I would have learned to be more than a little cautious in judging the spiritual motivation of any person who claims Christ as his Savior. Our Lord Jesus gives us the touchstone of truth: "By their fruits ye shall know them!" (Matt. 7:20).

7.

The Call Grows Clearer

Back from the second Caribbean tour, I was again on the road in the states, holding church campaigns and youth rallies. Summers were filled with Bible teaching at conferences, in the East, the South and the Midwest. I was seldom at home to help Ruth with the care of four lively little children—Martha, David, and the twins Joey and Jimmy—besides the special needs of our eldest, twelve-year-old Ruth Ellyn, who had cystic fibrosis. Yet my beloved family was never out of my mind, and when the opportunity came to take a great leap of faith in our little invalid's behalf, I grasped at it. I knew that *some* people had been healed by the Lord supernaturally in modern times, and I was so desperately anxious to help our suffering child that I was ready to be called a heretic or a fool. I would investigate even the slightest chance that God might grant a miracle.

Ruth Ellyn was a delicate flower in the garden of our Heavenly Father. From earliest childhood she had known and loved Jesus her Lord with the effortless faith that He often gives His "little ones"; and she was surrounded every moment by her parents' love. Her affliction made her seem younger than her twelve years, and her eyes held a beauty seldom seen in any child. They were full of light, deepened by suffering, yet always ready to sparkle with laughter.

Alone with her mother so much of the time, Ruth Ellyn thought and talked more like a grown-up than like a twelve-year-old. She showed no small talent for music and drawing, but it was heartbreaking to see how quickly her thin little body would droop, how soon she had to stop and rest. On my brief visits home between army camp tours and evangelical campaigns, her nightly paroxysms of coughing tore my heart. But what spirit she had! What bounce! When each strangling coughing spell ended she was as cheerful again as if nothing had happened.

At times, when she was able to attend school, she would come home crying brokenly. Thoughtless boys and girls had poked fun at her spindly legs, had sneered because she couldn't play strenuous games. We would hold her close and dry her tears, asking God for grace to forgive those who had hurt our delicate flower. The Bible speaks of being made "perfect through sufferings," but it also tells of Jesus healing the multitudes in His great compassion. The possibility of miraculous healing for our little sufferer was never out of our thoughts.

I was conducting a campaign in a church pastored by my youngest brother, Ben, when I began hearing table talk about Kathryn Kuhlman, who held meetings regularly at Carnegie Hall in Pittsburgh. When I referred to her as a "healer," I was promptly and politely corrected. Kathryn Kuhlman was *not* a "healer." She disclaimed any special power, and had no healing lines.

I was interested at once. "Then how do people get healed?" I asked Mrs. Lauffer, a woman with an outstanding Christian testimony, who was serving as an usher in Kathryn's meetings.

"Some receive healing from the Lord while in their seats; others are healed outside, while waiting for the doors to open," she answered me.

"Have you actually seen some of these so-called healings—up close?" I persisted.

"Of course! I know that they are not 'so-called' healings," she said matter-of-factly. "I have seen goiters disappear and crippled legs become straight, right beside me, as I stood in the aisle."

I turned to look at Ben. He declared his absolute confidence in Mrs. Lauffer's integrity, and he verified her account of how the meetings were conducted.

I began listening to Kathryn's messages on the radio. Her voice was confident and warm. I could spot no false doctrine or evidence of fraud, and I learned that she had been holding meetings in Pittsburgh for years. She would have been run out of town long ago if she had been guilty of deception.

I recognized that Kathryn Kuhlman was glorifying Jesus Christ as the Lord Who in love meets *all* of our needs, spiritual and physical. She emphasized that, while the saving of the soul was infinitely more important than the healing of the body, bodily healing often brought entire families to Christ, along with their friends.

Slowly my prejudices crumbled. I became convinced that God heals, not just to prove that He can, but because He is moved with compassion for the sick and afflicted in any age. Before I left Pittsburgh, I had made up my mind to return with Ruth Ellyn at the first opportunity—and so I did! The child's cough was growing worse, but between paroxysms, as we drove west on the turnpike, she laughed and talked happily.

Kathryn Kuhlman's meetings were held only once a week, at Carnegie Hall, and I knew that my own crowded schedule would not allow us to repeat this venture. In my heart was a crushing burden of sorrow, uncertainty, and desperate hope. *Would God heal our little girl?*

At last we were in the hall, and seated—in the front row of the balcony. Ruth Ellyn was impressed by the great crowd around her and by the beautiful music. Suddenly Kathryn Kuhlman was before us, greeting her audience. She was charming, without self-consciousness. She radiated good spirits, and her musical team gave her buoyant support.

But all at once I realized that this was not going to be a healing service! Kathryn was presenting a lovely red rose to each of a hundred or more gentlemen who filed across the platform. This was a Father's Day rally!

Kathryn's message, after the presentation of roses, was not on the subject of healing; and my desperate hope in making this trip had come to nothing. On the way home I tried to hide my feelings from Ruthie Ellyn, who in no way shared my depression. Why, I asked God, did things turn out this way?

Even today, I am not sure of the right answer. Sharp-edged questions remain. The four men who brought their paralytic friend to Jesus would not have given up so easily as I did. They tore up the roof tiles, so as to lower the sufferer to Jesus' feet. I know now that diseases worse and farther advanced than Ruth Ellyn's have been healed miraculously by our Savior; their case histories have been thoroughly verified by reputable doctors and by X rays. Had my indoctrinated unbelief in modern miracles crippled my *ability* to believe for Ruth Ellyn's healing? Had I failed her, or would her healing at this time have conflicted with the better plans of her infinitely loving Lord?

I only know that, years later, when Ruth Ellyn died, God restored to health my son Joey, after a distinguished specialist in Argentina told me, "This child cannot possibly live." Years later, we anointed with oil our other twin, Jimmy, and prayed, and he was miraculously healed. Jimmy had been in severe pain for six months, and once he had cried brokenly, "Why don't they send me to Vietnam so I can die?" Two days after we laid hands on him and prayed as they did in Bible times, the splotches on his skin disappeared, and in one week he was completely well.

I am sure that more people would be divinely healed if great numbers of us Christians had real faith for it. The *reality* of faith is what counts, according to our Lord, even if it be "as a grain of mustard seed."

While I was still following a busy schedule of meetings, there came an invitation from the Latin America missions to go to Argentina and Uruguay as a guest artist. Two Central American evangelists, Eliseo Hernandez, from El Salvador, and Israel Garcia of Costa Rica, had been signed up; Juan Isais would lead the singing, and Bill and Pearl Thompson would head the team.

I felt God's leading very clearly. As soon as possible I put my passport and related papers in order, reconstructed my easel, and joined the others. Bill had no way of knowing how men used to the tropics would thrive in the cooler and drier air of Argentina, so he planned for two evangelists, in case one of them should chance to be "under the weather." Bill, a longtime veteran on the field, could have preached, but he preferred to put the Latin Americans forward. We went first to Uruguay.

Despite my two years of Spanish at Wheaton College, I found it difficult to follow rapid Spanish in conversation or preaching; however, my job was to draw, usually while somebody else sang. When I did sing, in English, our audiences seemed to enjoy it. They liked it, too, when I did quick sketches, explained by interpretation.

Once, preaching about David killing Goliath, I staggered back like the stricken giant—and my interpreter, Theda Krieger, copied me so exactly that for a moment I thought we would end in a heap on the floor!

After campaigning for several weeks in Uruguay, we held our first Argentine meeting in the large auditorium of the evangelical church of Villa Real, where Don José Bangarra was the spiritual leader. It required no little daring for Don José to include me in the program, since many Christians in this area could not imagine how chalk pictures could possibly glorify the Lord. Today there are still a few closed minds that hold that drawing with colored chalks "da gusto a la carne" (glorifies the flesh)!

Too many meetings in Argentina at that time were forced into a preset religious form which robbed them of freshness and vigor. Worse still, it hindered the free working of God's Holy Spirit. I recall a typical service where our team waited through several numbers by a choir, a lengthy scripture reading, a long prayer, half-a-dozen hymns (all seven or ten verses sung by the congregation) and some detailed announcements—before we were given our part in the program.

I whispered to Bill Thompson, "If this keeps up much longer, I'm not going to draw. It wouldn't be fair to the evangelist or to this tired crowd, to keep them so late."

"Now, Phil," Bill whispered back, "this is the way they do things down here."

I must have replied with a bit of heat; but Bill was reminding me of a very difficult problem facing an "extranjero" from overseas: Where should he draw the line between customs to be respected and customs to be ignored?

At that time, following World War II, there was still a strong pro-Axis sentiment among the Argentines, and some very real antagonism toward the United States, for large segments of the population were of German or Italian origin. Many of these had relatives who had suffered terribly under Allied bombing. So it was, when we were in Rosario, planning for meetings in Cordoba, five hours away, some people said it wouldn't be safe for me to go.

I went, however, and nothing untoward occurred. What did happen was that God called me to be a full-time missionary to live in that city, making it my permanent base of operations on the mission field.

The call was so strong that I spoke of it from the platform, through an interpreter. What I said drew incredulous smiles from members of my own team; but the friendly Argentine Christians who packed the Sociedad Española rejoiced. Many of them began then and there to pray for me, asking God to open the way for my return.

Several facts had prepared me for this call. One was that ninety percent of gospel preachers were ministering to ten percent of the world's people. In the states I often found myself in a city church holding meetings in competition with another evangelist only a few blocks away. A painful contrast with the lack of gospel witness in other lands! Moreover, in Argentina and Uruguay I had found a dearth of first-rate musicians available for Christian meetings; and the eagerness of the people to see Bible themes drawn in color was far greater in these countries than at home.

Of less importance were some personal considerations that pointed in the same direction. The dry climate of Cordoba would be kind to our invalid daughter; and the Spanish language, which has 5,000 words cognate with English ones, would be much easier to learn than any other. I had noticed that even the dogs in Argentina understood Spanish when commanded to come, go, or lie down! This convinced me that I could learn it, too.

When I went over all this with Ruth, she began at once to pray and prepare for our move. Actually her basic decision had been made long ago.

One day, before we were married, we had been sitting alone under the elms of Wheaton's beautiful campus. Ruth had looked at me, and with the same depth of feeling that must have moved her namesake, Ruth the Moabitess, she quoted: "Whither thou goest, I will go; and where thou lodgest I will lodge: Thy people shall be my people, and thy God my God: Where thou diest I will die, and there will I be buried: The Lord do so to me, and more also, if ought but death part thee and me" (Ruth 1:16–17).

She meant it then, and I knew she hadn't changed. I also knew that when we went, we would go to stay—never returning to the states to retire. We would stay in Argentina until Jesus came back again, or we were called into His glorious presence. At the time I could not possibly imagine it would be only a short time before two Saints would be buried in the soil of South America— one in a quiet, shaded cemetery in Cordoba, the other along the banks of the wild Curaray River in the rain forest of Ecuador.

Before our move to Argentina I held a missionary rally in a northern city. As I was preaching, the Lord led me to mention that I was going to South America as a full-time missionary, *despite* my age. I was then forty-two—rather too old for a missionary board to consider. Among my hearers was a talented children's worker. She sat bolt upright, saying to herself, "Why, I'm forty-two! And if Phil Saint can go to the foreign field in spite of his age, what's to hinder me?"

This lady's daughter, recently married, did not need her; and her husband had left her, saying angrily, "I didn't marry a religious fanatic, and I'm not going to live with one!" There was really nothing to hinder her call. Today this consecrated woman is a child evangelism leader in Spanish-speaking America.

It is always the case that when we step out by faith, others are challenged to follow, and this will continue until Jesus our Lord comes back again.

I had thought of going directly to Argentina from the United States, but this was not to be. All the tedious paper work for our entry was lost with the overthrow of the dictator, Juan Peron. Nothing could be done about getting residence visas until new government officials were installed, so we went to language school in Costa Rica, where we should have planned to go in the first place. Again, God's hand was directing our paths. If we had gone directly to Argentina, I would surely have been caught up in other activities than language study, and might not have mastered Spanish for many years.

Our home in Greensboro, North Carolina, where we had moved, was in a whirl of sorting and packing for the trip—an orderly whirl, thanks to Ruth's deft management. I was in and out of the place, holding meetings, informing friends of our call to Argentina. Needed funds began coming in; and soon, after the difficult farewells had been said, we were on a plane bound for Miami and thence across the Gulf to Central America. San José, Costa Rica, was our destination.

From our plane the city appeared like a glowing jewel nestled in green velvet. On landing we found it a flower-scented paradise. At four thousand feet above sea level, it is never too hot or too chilly. The sun shines even during the rainy season. The city's atmosphere is cosmopolitan and colorful. Even the poorer citizens sport bright shirts and jackets.

Living and studying among Costa Rica's friendly people was going to be a glorious experience. I knew that, but I had not counted on the awful frustration of not being able to preach! After twenty-odd years as an evangelist, I was as effectively gagged as if I had lockjaw, and there was no quick way to cross the language barrier.

Months before leaving the states, I had listened to Spanish tapes as I drove from one meeting to another; but while I was gaining some familiarity with the tones and accents of Spanish, I understood few of the rapidly spoken words. Here, among Latins, I was still grasping at words carried too swiftly past me on the currents of conversation.

Ruth and I rented a place a few blocks from our language school. It was complete with a thick carpet of green lawn, a beautiful collie dog, and a little maid-of-all-work who was scarcely

taller than Ruth Ellyn. We enrolled the children in a fine grammar school, not too far away.

Our study center numbered more than a hundred students
drawn from many denominations. Most were evangelicals although a few followed the "modern" trend in theology which im-
pugned the authority of the Holy Bible. One of my teachers was
from Colombia. He had been both a pastor and an evangelist in
that country's interior at a time of religious ferment, when evangelical Christians were being severely persecuted. His fiery zeal
was contagious, and sometimes explosive. In the middle of a lesson the recollection of a thrilling experience in Colombia would
suddenly bring him to his feet with an eloquent flood of Spanish
that was too rapid for us beginners. He was dramatic, and at times
whimsical. Once, contrasting the English temperament with the
Spanish, he gave us this illustration:

An Englishman concludes that he would like to kill a "toro" in
a bullring; so he calls a meeting of his business acquaintances and
tells them of his decision. They talk endlessly over cups of tea.
They organize a corporation, sell stock, make reports, attend to
other business; and, some years later, they finally get around to
the bullfight.

"The Latin," declared our teacher, "bypasses all tiresome planning. He rushes into the arena. 'Stand back, everybody!' he
shouts. 'I'm going to kill the bull!' "

Our instructor had a pertinent epigram: "The British think;
the North Americans do; the Latins *feel.*" It pointed up the fact
that a method highly effective in the states might be the worst
possible choice in South America. Traditions, customs, and temperament are all so different, and they affect all communication,
even in art. In sculpture the typical Anglo-Saxon motif often uses
dominant, straight lines. Its beauty is formal, immobile, whereas
Latin sculpture is dynamic, expressing struggle and mobility. A
flaming spirit is caught, but never quenched, in stone. Even the

gentler themes of motherhood or of peace, in Latin America, seem to breathe into marble or bronze the deep feeling of the sculptor.

At language school, Ruth and I became fast friends with Paul and Madalyn Wegmueller, veteran missionaries, lately from Cuba. They had come to Costa Rica for some refresher courses, but Madalyn's class work was interrupted by an acute onset of chronic undulant fever. Periodically, the disease would prostrate her, and the fever would climb to dangerous levels. Spells of frightful shaking accompanied the fever. Despite every care at the "Clinica Biblica," a fine hospital founded and operated by the Latin America Missions, Madalyn grew worse and worse. It seemed that she might die at any time.

A number of the language students decided to go to the hospital and offer special prayer for her healing. These young men had confidence in God's power and willingness to heal; moreover, they believed they had God's assurance that He was going to answer their prayer of faith. Feeling no such assurance, but only a desperate hope, I went along.

First, we knelt in a separate room and prayed earnestly. Then we filed into the sickroom, where Madalyn lay pale and deathly still. After weeks of steady decline, she was obviously nearing the end. At her bedside, several of our group prayed, and we anointed her with oil in the Name of the Lord. Then we left.

From that hour, Madalyn began to improve. Within two weeks she was out of the hospital, and at this writing she is on the mission field with her husband, in Venezuela.

Spanish is not difficult if one is content to slide along, learning just enough to buy groceries and get around from place to place. But to stand before intelligent, cultured Latin audiences and preach fluently with all of the beautiful, compelling modes of speech of which this great language is capable—that is quite another matter. Ruth and I tremble to think how our ministry in

South America would have been crippled if we had not come to this language school in Costa Rica.

Mr. and Mrs. Otho La Porte were called of God to conduct this study center while they were in a Japanese concentration camp in the Philippines during World War II. Thanks to their faithfulness, we, and a hundred others, were making headway through a turbulent sea of radical changing verbs, pseudoprincipal clauses, elliptical contrary-to-fact conditions, perfect and imperfect subjunctives, modal auxiliaries, diminutives and augmentatives, and similar baffling forms. How I envied our five children, who, in a few weeks, were chattering away in Spanish to their little Costa Rican friends. The language just soaked in through their pores!

Almost as important as learning the Latin American language and culture was getting to know the religious tides that flowed about us. On Good Friday afternoon, I felt drawn to the center of San José, to see for myself what Holy Week ceremonies in Central America were like.

A mammoth crowd of perhaps fifteen thousand had been waiting in front of the great cathedral for two hours in the hot tropical sun; for all of them had been taught from childhood that it would be sinful not to be present at the funeral of "our Lord." Finally a bugler appeared at the top of the cathedral steps. He blew a long-drawn, high-pitched note which seemed to last a full minute. When he had ended, forty men in dark suits, with purple sashes across their chests, came out of the great doors. A military band followed them, playing a sepulchral dirge. Next came an altar boy, swinging a censer. Its pungent, heavy odor filled the air. Several priests in black robes and oddly shaped hats moved slowly behind a golden casket, which was very ornate and closed in with glass panels. The stony expression on each clerical face lent a touch of weirdness to the scene, even before I saw clearly what was inside the casket.

There, beneath a transparent lace veil, appeared the startlingly realistic corpse of Christ. Its head hung limply back, and its mouth was open in a ghastly expression of death. Blood streaked the pale, waxlike face.

Close behind was borne the image of the "Blessed Virgin, Mother of God." Her delicate features held a look of unutterable grief, which seemed to be reflected by the sad-faced women who lined the way. It was *their* look which tore my heart! And close behind the Virgin's image surged a sea of mournful worshipers.

On Easter Sunday I returned downtown between five and six in the morning, because I had heard that the figure of the Risen Christ would be carried back to the Cathedral along the same route taken by the Good Friday procession. To my surprise, the streets were almost deserted. Where, I wondered, were the fifteen thousand people who had waited in the hot sun two days ago?

At last I saw activity, far down a narrow street. The group was coming with the statue of the resurrected Christ. They were mostly in their shirtsleeves, some without neckties. They walked rapidly, as if hurrying through a perfunctory task. A scattering of musicians trailed them, marching to a noisy, ragtime tune imported from the states.

"O God," I prayed out of a broken heart, "help me to learn Spanish well, so that I can tell these dear people about a living Savior Who stands ready to lift them "out of darkness into His marvelous light!"

8.

More than Conquerors!

We were still at language school when the first vague rumors of trouble in Ecuador began to reach us. For a day or two there was nothing definite; but apparently there had been a plane accident, involving my brother Nate, a missionary pilot. Then came the blow, the bare, grim facts. Nate, with four more young missionaries, had been killed by the Auca Indians.

My first impulse was to fly there at once, on a chance that I might be of help; on second thought, I pictured people swarming all over Shell Mera, the last outpost of civilization, where Nate had been based. When I got word that my elder brother Sam, an American Airlines pilot, had flown there, and that my sister Rachel was at Shell Mera with the martyrs' families, I decided to stay in school. In a highly accelerated language program like ours, the loss of even one week could leave me far behind.

Deeply moved, Ruth and I solemnly renewed our dedication to the cause of winning those in other lands to Christ. Nate, twelve years younger than I but already a veteran missionary, had been called suddenly from his work; our work was here, and now. Yet thoughts of my kid brother, the finest of us all, kept crowding my most determined efforts to study. Vivid memories of his childhood, his growing-up years, his youthful struggles and victories, swept over me, day and night.

When he was very little, Nate was such a beautiful child that passersby would stop Mother in the street to admire her son. It was not just because of his blond hair and rosy cheeks, or his big blue eyes that mirrored the sky he loved even then; it was rather the expression on his features that caught people's attention, a look that spoke of a brilliant, beautiful mind and spirit. So much admiration made little Nate very shy, so that at times, when visitors came to the house, he hid under the bed until they had left.

Soon after big brother Sam got his pilot's license, he took Nate up for his first flight. The child had to sit on a box in order to see out of the cockpit, but that day he drank in the full wonder of soaring flight. Nothing escaped him, and from that day on, piloting a plane was his great ambition.

Adolescence changed him into a slat-thin, angular youth with a Scotch-Irish nose. By this time he was servicing planes in a huge hangar-factory, during the Second World War, and with each passing year his love of the skies deepened. Often he would find an excuse to step outside, just to look up for a few moments at the vast blue sky and dream of flying. He fretted at the confinement of shop work, but this was a God-directed preparation for the time when, as a jungle pilot, he would have to be his own mechanic.

When the chance came to try out for Air Force flight training, Nate eagerly registered, and came out sixth from the top among hundreds who took the examinations. Suddenly, just before he was due to leave for training in Texas, an old bone infection which had plagued him in childhood recurred. Slivers of bone began working themselves out to the surface of his shin. Instead of going to flight school, Nate went to the hospital.

There, suffering intense pain, and a worse agony of disappointment, my kid brother began fighting the hardest spiritual battle of his life. In his misery he was tempted to believe that God had forsaken him. He felt that he had been born to fly, but now, Satan whispered, it was all over. God had allowed this illness to mock him!

The battle continued after he had left the hospital, the struggle between despair and his love for God. One winter night, as Nate wandered aimlessly through Detroit's snowy streets, it ended. Nate prayed, "Lord, if it's Your will that I never fly again, it's okay with me."

Flying set aside, Nate was soon enrolled at Wheaton College, preparing for full-time Christian work. In his spare time he taught young boys the Bible and tried to win them to Christ. Soul winning was now his first and only concern. But soon God, Who had demanded that Nate Saint surrender the great desire of his life, to be a flyer, all at once gave it back to him.

He learned of a missionary organization, the Missionary Aviation Fellowship, which used small planes to open up out-of-the-way places in the foreign field. Immediately he got in touch with Grady Parrott and other members of this group. Without waiting to finish college, he entered the Moody Bible Institute flight training school to prepare for joining the M.A.F. Soon he would be carrying the life-giving Good News of his Savior to forgotten savage tribesmen—instead of dropping lethal bombs on enemy targets!

Nate had learned something of the cost of complete discipleship from the example of our dedicated parents. He was to learn still more. A plane crash in Ecuador put him in the hospital, temporarily blind, and with a broken back. I shall never forget what he said then: "If I must be blind and crippled the rest of my life in order that Indians may be saved, it is worth it all!"

As the shock of his injury wore off, Nate's sight returned, and while still wearing the plaster cast that encased him from neck to thighs, he was back again in the jungles, building an advance mission base and a crude airstrip. At times the blazing sun made his cast so hot that he had to hunt shade and pour water down inside his plaster shell to keep from being burned.

How Nate met and married Marj, his talented, gracious wife, has been told in the book, *Jungle Pilot*. God knew how much Nate would need her loving, strong support when he faced the great hardships ahead. He made daily flights, alert for menacing cloud formations above trackless forests, knowing there was no place to land in case of trouble. Nate lived with danger every day for seven years, and the tensions of his work etched deep lines on his face. When he was with us briefly, about a year before his death, and I was helping him splice together a film of jungle Indians, our neighbors thought he was much older than I!

Marj was his nurse when he was sick, his radio operator when he was flying. She mothered and taught their three small children in the wilderness, and she fully shared Nate's sense of mission.

There was no recklessness, no taint of bravado, in my brother. Methodical and meticulous in everything, he was always figuring out some new device to make missionary aviation safer, more efficient. His previously unheard-of trick of lowering a bucket or a basket on a rope (to make contact with savages on the ground), while flying in a tight circle, has captured the imagination of topflight aviation engineers. Not once, but five times, Nate landed his small plane on the impossibly short river beach where he and his companions were to die, pierced by Auca spears. He had measured the length of the landing place ("Palm Beach") from the air by dropping bags of colored dust at split-second intervals and then counting the splotches.

After the killers had done their horrible work, and when rescue planes were circling overhead, an American army pilot looked down incredulously at tiny "Palm Beach." "Nobody," he muttered to himself —"but *nobody*—could land on a beach like that!"

I have watched the film of one of Nate's earlier landings there, and have been awed by the smooth grace of his plane as it followed the curve of the river, and sideslipped in for the touchdown—a wing almost brushing the trees and the opposite wheel just missing the water! Nate and his plane had become one—the machine obeying with perfect precision its pilot's will.

When the first news of the massacre reached us we could only guess what had brought the five young missionaries together on that fatal beach. "Operation Auca" had been kept secret from everybody but the martyrs' wives.

There were good reasons for this secrecy. Achieving even one friendly contact with a group of ferocious, suspicious, and utterly primitive Auca Indians was generally believed to be impossible. Both government and Shell Oil personnel dreaded these killers, who would appear from the forest gloom with phantom suddenness, armed with long razor-sharp spears of iron-hard *chonta* palm. Aucas had slaughtered foreigners and Ecuadorian soldiers—and had suffered casualties from high-powered rifles. It was known that murder was a part of the Aucas' social pattern, forcing them to live in small, mutually hostile communities. For hundreds of years they had attacked every stranger who had dared to enter their forests. The headhunting Jívaros and the Quechua-speaking Indians had always feared them. Now, however, the forerunners of civilization, map makers and oil scouts, were infringing on Auca territory and alarming the savages. If these exploring teams, not to mention a concerned and alert government, had gotten wind of the young missionaries' project, it might have incited them to competitive efforts—and the Aucas to more "defensive" killings. The hope for any friendly contact would have been gone.

"Operation Auca" was months in planning and preparation, hedged about with earnest prayer. The dangers were surmountable only if Almighty God were directing every detail, as the young men prayed for guidance. From September till January, Nate Saint made flight after flight over the little Auca village that he had discovered in a clearing, near a branch of the Curaray River. The missionaries lowered gifts in a basket, as Nate flew a tight circle high above. Each week they made a visit, lowering machetes, kettles, bright shirts, trinkets, trousers. Once an Auca tied a bag containing a live parrot onto the dangling rope—a "thank-you" token? At any rate the villagers appeared pleased with their gifts.

Face-to-face contact might be much more difficult. Certainly it would be dangerous. From years of experience with other tribes, Nate and his friends knew that a savage may receive a gift dropped from the skies with childish pleasure—and ferociously resent any personal intrusion into his territory. They knew also that the Aucas had good reason to hate white men. "Civilized" whites had burned their huts to the ground, shot their men ruthlessly, and carried off their women. It is said that neighboring tribes in times past captured Aucas for cannibalistic feasts, so suspicion marked every stranger, white or red, as a potential man-eater. If not a cannibal, today's intruder would still compete for the forest's all too scanty food sources. If for no other reason, he would thus be an enemy, to be killed.

All five of the young missionaries knew this. They knew something else, of far greater importance: that the blood of God's Son, Jesus Christ, was shed "for every man," including every Auca. They saw these Stone-Age killers bound for spiritual as well as physical death, but capable of being reborn to spiritual life, through knowing God's love. Of this love they must be told—at any cost!

They made five landings on "Palm Beach" near the Auca village, beginning January 2, bringing radio, walkie-talkie, tools, food, boards, and sheets of aluminum to build a shelter. They made a camp, caught and cooked fish, broadcast their memorized

Auca phrases: "I like you!" and such. They prayed, and with the help of insect repellent, they slept.

On Friday, January 6, Nate's diary records, they met their first Aucas face-to-face—a man and two women, naked except for their G-strings. The three waded across the shallow river, and Jim Elliot led them to the others, who laughed and smiled and welcomed their visitors, in newly learned Auca phrases. The Indians chatted happily in their own tongue. They seemed entirely unafraid and showed a childlike curiosity about everything.

Nate showed them the plane, and persuaded the man to go for a ride. Actually, he got two rides—one, just a brief circle over the beach; the other, a swing over his village, wearing a bright-colored gift shirt. He shouted with pleasure and excitement all the way there and back.

As with children, the Aucas' curiosity was easily satisfied. They drifted back into the forest, and the missionaries knew that it would be unwise to follow them. They hoped and prayed that, before long, others of the tribe would appear with an invitation to visit their village.

The next day, Saturday, no Aucas came, but Nate flew to the home base at Shell Mera with films and photos of the Friday visitors and left them with Marj. He was back to keep vigil with his four companions on the river beach that night. His diary tells that he lay awake until one o'clock, wondering how they might have kept their Friday callers around longer, and whether fear was making the others stay away.

On Sunday, January 8, Nate took a "short flight" over the Auca *chacra* and noted that no men were in sight. A little after noon, he used his plane's radio to call the base and say, "We're hoping for visitors at about 2:30. I'll call you again at 4:35."

At 4:35 there was silence. Marj waited in vain. When it became certain that something was very wrong, a plane was sent to investigate. It reported that the missionaries' plane had been demolished, and that a body was floating in the river.

Several other missionaries, together with some guides and a detail of Ecuadorian soldiers, started afoot for the scene of the tragedy. The United States Air Force Rescue Service sent planes at once from Panama. One of their pilots, Major Malcom Nurnberg, located four bodies downriver from the beach and later joined the other searchers there. The fifth body, that of Ed McCulley, was not found, but an Indian from his mission base found one of his large sneakers.

In the four bodies recovered, decomposition was far advanced. Laundry marks on their clothing and the contents of their pockets identified them. Jim Elliot, Pete Fleming, Roger Youderian, Ed McCulley, and Nate Saint had joined the great company of martyrs for the cause of Christ.

Frank Drown, who led the missionary contingent of the search party, began digging a common grave for the five men. Others tried to salvage small parts from the plane that the killers had wrecked in their murderous frenzy.

The humid heat and their own emotions had left the burial party exhausted, but the jungle had one more brutal slap for them. As they laid their dead friends' pitiful remains in the grave, the bright sunlight was snuffed out. The roar of a tropical rainstorm drowned out all other sound. Hastily the grave was filled and covered with aluminum sheets from the demolished tree house as Major Nurnberg sprayed the surrounding jungle with machine-gun bursts to protect the party from possible attack. While soldiers peered through the darkness, half-expecting a rush of shadowy spearmen, the missionaries hurried through a simple burial service.

Next morning, after a wretched night spent in the middle of Auca territory, they started back . . .

At Shell Mera, it was Dr. Johnston's heartbreaking task to tell the martyrs' wives what they had found, and done. When the

bare, terrible facts were told, the women raised together the
hymn that their husbands had sung before entering Auca Land:

> *"We rest on Thee, our Shield and our Defender;*
> *Thine is the battle, Thine shall be the praise.*
> *When passing through the gates of pearly splendor,*
> *Victors, we rest with Thee through endless days."*

Critics have suggested that Nate and his four companions
misjudged the Indians and the risk that they were taking, but I
believe that all five men knew far more about what they were
doing than any "armchair authorities" could possibly know. They
had good reason to hope that the friendliness of the Aucas with
whom they had made contact, both from the plane and later face-
to-face, would set a pattern for future meetings. And this hope
would very likely have been realized, as we learned much later,
had not enmity suddenly erupted between Naenkiwi (the man
who visited the missionaries on Friday) and the other men of the
Auca community. When Naenkiwi, on Sunday, went to visit the
strangers again, tribal rage spilled over to include the outsiders.

Nate Saint and his friends knew from the start that the unexpected might happen—they might be killed. They took firearms
along to frighten the savages, but they all determined never to fire
at an Indian, not even in self-defense. Their mission was to tell,
and to exemplify, Christ's love. Years afterward we learned from
an eyewitness that the five martyrs had fired their guns into the
air and, unresisting, let themselves be speared.

They had planned carefully, praying over every detail. After
their deaths, an army officer commented that he had never seen a
military campaign carried through with more care and foresight.
"Those fellows thought of everything," he declared.

God could have called a halt to "Operation Auca" at any point,
as He could have prevented the stoning to death of the New Testament martyr, Stephen. He didn't, because these men would ac-

complish most toward the salvation of priceless souls by dying as they did. They jolted the conscience of millions, around the world, as their story was blazed in newspapers and magazines, by radio and television. Their relatives, scores of them, gave testimony before large audiences to the young men's selfless motives. Scores of missionaries and missionary candidates have told me personally that their call to the foreign field resulted directly from the martyrdom of these five. By their deaths God opened the way for Betty Elliot, little Valerie, and my sister Rachel to go in among the very Indians who did the killing.

Rachel and Dayuma (the Auca girl who dared to guide her there in 1958) stayed on. At this writing they have the joy of continuing to teach and train over seventy-five baptized Auca believers. Several of these have become true spiritual leaders. Members of this jungle tribe are ready to lay down their lives for Christ. That is the picture today, and I know that Nate and his speared friends could have wished for no greater reward.

Some time after the massacre, I was told that Abe Van der Puy of HCJB, the famous missionary radio station at Quito, had been decorated as representing the martyrs, by the President of Ecuador.

9.

The Saints Arrive in Argentina

On March 15, 1957, our family arrived by plane at the Ezeiza International Airport of Buenos Aires. Several friends were there to meet us, among them Don José Bongarrá, an outstanding Christian leader, who helped us to get through the customs. At last we were in Argentina as permanent residents!

After a few days in the great capital we went by train to Cordoba, at the geographic center of the country—a twelve-hour trip. We crossed the great plains at night, and were met at the station by John Clifford, another prominent evangelical. John helped us load our boxes and bales into two dilapidated horse-drawn *mateos* which must have been quite elegant back in the nineteenth century. Cordoba, in 1957, was a city of strong contrasts, partly old and partly new, just waking up from agelong slumber.

Since the main avenue was under repair, we had to jolt along narrow, cobblestoned back streets, stopping now and then to give a little old-fashioned trolley car the right of way. It was all very picturesque, but with every jolt and halt I asked myself, "What have I—and my poor family—gotten into?"

When we finally arrived at the Cliffords' home, their pleasant rooms, their good food, and above all, their warm hospitality, banished my qualms. It couldn't have been easy for them to find beds and bedding for the seven of us, but they appeared to have done it without feeling the slightest inconvenience.

The next day we were taken to a lovely cottage nestled among abrupt, rocky hills, and here my family stayed while I went looking for a house to buy in the city. I lost no time in starting, but getting to downtown Cordoba took a lot of time. I had to take a bus into a country town and wait there for another one to the city, where I arrived just as everything shut down for the three-hour siesta. Sitting out those three hours in a park was a hard lesson in patience for a man who has always been in a hurry.

When the town woke up again, and I could ask directions, I met another frustration: Argentine Spanish idioms! They include some colorful expressions that any South American visitor would probably understand, but which I couldn't figure out at all. To make things harder, many streets had historic dates for names, and Cordobans, offering to direct me, would leave off the word for "avenue," just giving me the date!

Obviously I could have looked for weeks or months to find a suitable place to live, but the Lord led me on the very first day to the spacious old house where we were to live happily for many years. When I saw the large front yard and the big living room, I thought immediately of open-air meetings, and of starting a local church. There should be time for this, before I could get into the full swing of evangelistic work.

Many Argentine homes are built up close to the street, with a patio in the rear, for privacy, but this was an old style house. Its situation just suited me, but inside it was frightful. The old, stooped grandmother and the half-wit girl who lived with her showed me through the untidy rooms. They had all been painted the same color, with the cheapest water paint; and they had apparently been constructed without any clear plan. I could see attractive possibilities through the shambles, and I hoped that Ruth would be able to bring order out of it when she took over.

Happily she did. We made an ample dining room by taking out a partition between two small rooms. A new hallway permitted access to it without going through a bedroom. The kitchen had to be done over completely, from something that looked like a stable. The place had been on the market for two years—a white elephant.

When the deal went through we had acquired altogether five lots and a large old house, with big, beautiful trees, all for less than four thousand dollars. The money came from the sale of our lovely home in Greensboro, N.C., so there has been no rent or mortgage to pay for our residence on the mission field, and the property we bought is worth today many times what we paid for it.

The bulk of our belongings came later, by boat from the states. Since they were all used articles, the duty on them was negligible, but customs negotiations seemed to go on endlessly. Still, every ordeal has an end. With the last needed signature in hand, and a big rented truck waiting at the warehouse door for our barrels and boxes, I started to breathe freely. Then came the final hitch.

A customs official took the top off a barrel and pulled out one of the porcelain plates of a dinner set that Mom Brooker had given us. He held it up to the light, tapped it with his thumbnail, and said, "*¡Porcelana, porcelana! Los papeles no dicen nada de porcelana.*" (The papers say nothing about porcelain.) Plainly, he intended to hold up the entire shipment until next day, in order to charge me duty on those dishes.

With the truck rented and ready, I was caught, but I laughed. "Look, señor," I replied, "those dishes were given us by my mother-in-law. Let's just toss them into the harbor and forget them."

The man's thought was plain in his puzzled expression: "These North Americans are crazy!" He put the plate back in the barrel, closed the lid, and waved to the *peones* to cart off everything to our waiting truck.

In a short time we had prayer meetings going in our living room, and soon, despite my limited ability in Spanish, we had fifty or sixty neighbors crowding in to hear the gospel. When summer came, I put together a small platform, strung a few lights from tree to tree, and we began outdoor meetings. Most people in our area were respectful, but there was one huge, shapeless old character who, when drunk, would ride by on his horse, waving a liquor bottle and shouting insults at the *evangelicos.* Some young bloods threatened to beat up any other youths who dared to attend.

Another neighbor, curious but fanatically opposed to our gospel program, hopped onto his bicycle and pedaled furiously away at the first sound of singing. He came back when the meeting was over to find a group in our open driveway, studying the last chalk picture. He joined them. When told that I had done the scene in less than fifteen minutes, he couldn't believe it, and the next evening he was lurking behind a tree on the other side of the street to watch the chalk-drawing. Only when I picked up the Bible did he jump on his bicycle and disappear in a cloud of dust. But curiosity had him hooked! On the following night our off-again-on-again-gone-again visitor stayed through the preaching; and later in our local tent campaign he became one of our first converts.

Those humble beginnings developed into a full-blown church ministry. The local group took more and more responsibility, and I was able to move farther afield.

Not long after arriving in Argentina, I was invited to draw in meetings conducted by the famous evangelist, Dr. Oswald J. Smith, at Luna Park, the mammoth boxing stadium in Buenos Aires. This was one of the greatest opportunities to draw for

Christ that I had ever had. I hurriedly prepared a huge easel that could be clearly seen from the farthest row of seats.

When I entered Luna Park, the stadium's cavernous interior seemed dark after the bright sunlight outside. A few tattered workers were arranging chairs and sweeping up the debris left by the boxing fans the night before. The smell of stale tobacco smoke still hung in the air. Large billboards advertising alcoholic beverages were being taken down, and the *cabeza* of electric lights for the boxing ring had been pulled up among the steel girders. Several people helped me carry the big easel to the front of the gallery above the boxing ring, and set it up. It had special banks of colored lights with reinforced rheostats, to illuminate my over-size chalk pictures.

That night and every night, Luna Park was packed to the rafters. At times thirty thousand came, but only twenty-five thousand could get in. Dr. Smith, a slim, straight, white-haired figure, preached with simplicity and power. Each night I drew a feature picture on some related theme, moving from one side of the easel to the other, at times singing memorized hymns in Spanish, with a mike around my neck. The great choir led by missionary Bob Byler, and special songs by talented Argentines, deeply stirred the audience. At the invitation, people streamed down the aisles. All in all, there were over fifteen hundred first-time decisions for Christ; and many hundreds of Christians, challenged by Dr. Smith, reconsecrated themselves to the Lord.

More than a dozen years have passed since then, but I still meet people who remember the meetings led by that great man of God at Luna Park.

Dr. Smith invited me to go with him to Santiago, Chile. There a tremendous open-air stadium was jammed to overflowing, and hundreds came to the Savior. The splendid choir was led by Salomon Mussiett, who later joined our team in Argentina, and it was at the same time that I met Francisco Bilbao, one of the most gifted lyric tenors of our time. He, too, became a member of our team, traveling with us as our soloist.

During this campaign, Dr. Smith asked me to go with him to Lima, Peru. I told him that I would be happy to go, but that I had no money for flying with my big easel that far north. When this need was made known in the next meeting, they took up a special offering to cover it and turned over to me a huge cardboard carton packed with *pesos*. This was before Chile introduced the *escudo*, worth one thousand *pesos*. Counting the offering would take two or three people hours to finish, and the bulky paper in low denominations was hard to manage. So the next morning I took my problem to the bank.

When the teller saw my carton crammed full of bills he threw up his hands. "No, no, señor, we can't take care of all that!"

"Well," I replied, "Señor so-and-so (naming a nationally known industrialist who had directed me to the bank) promised that you would help me."

That changed matters. *"Bueno!"* exclaimed the teller. "Let me have it, but don't come back until late this afternoon."

When I returned, the mountain of bills had been made into a check which just nicely took me to Lima.

In Lima the evangelistic committee had rented an old circus tent. It was the most patched and faded piece of canvas I had ever seen, but it seated three thousand people and it was beautifully located. Thanks to energetic advertising, the entire city knew about the campaign, and the opening meetings were glorious. Joy and blessing ran like fire through the crowds. But on Friday night, with no warning, the police came, took up positions at all entrances, and shut us out. It appeared that some government official, giving way to antievangelical pressure, had declared the meetings to be "street meetings," which were not permitted to any except the state church.

Of course this was contrary to the spirit of religious liberty which usually prevails in Peru and most other South American countries, but since the next two days were a weekend, it was impossible to get the order rescinded until Monday, when the campaign would be over. Hurried arrangements were made for holding the final services in a partly completed church—did you ever try to fit three thousand people into an auditorium built for three hundred?

With the Lima campaign ended, Dr. Oswald Smith was on his way back to Canada, and I was flying across the snow-covered Andes range, back home to Argentina.

Even though I was over forty-two years of age, with considerable experience in conducting gospel meetings, this did not make me a mature or capable missionary. Some Argentine leaders who had seen me draw but had never heard me preach thought naturally that teaming up with one of their national orators would be an ideal arrangement for me. But God had called me to *preach* as well as to draw. Moreover, I knew that I would never master the language just *listening to* the most eloquent Argentine evangelist. For better or worse, I would have to do my own preaching. A fire was burning in my soul that could not be quenched by man-made plans. So, although I was severely criticized by some people for "wanting to do it all," and "be a big shot," I obeyed the voice of the Holy Spirit, and after several campaigns with national evangelists launched out on my own.

Inevitably I paid with many bumps and bruises for my independence; yet I learned faster this way, sparing no effort to adapt myself to the country and its people. The great circus tent in Lima had left a deep impression on me, and I began to pray that the Lord would one day give me such a means of bridging the gap between the gospel and the man in the street. Eventually, He did.

Moving into a tent ministry took time as well as funds. It involved not only a tent, but a way to transport it and to gain experience in its use. In the meantime, meetings must be held in a stadium or a large hall. Often we found that arrangements for such a place would mysteriously be canceled at the last minute, through "political" pressure to which a tent would have been less vulnerable.

Once we went to a teeming neighborhood, using a large platform truck and placing it across a dead-end street. By the time the organ and easel were set up and lights and loudspeaker equipment turned on, the street was jammed with onlookers. At the bottom of the street a trolley line bordered the main avenue. Each time one of the crowded, swaying little cars came to the intersection, it stopped, so that all of the passengers could watch the drawing and hear the music. And there it stayed until the next "Toonerville" came rocking along. "Clang! Clang! Clang!" the bell forced the first trolley to move on, leaving the next one to provide a momentary grandstand for its curious occupants.

If chalk drawings and music were attractions in a city, they were still more effective in places where television was unknown, and where local motion-picture shows left much to be desired. In one country town a man of the world was heard to say, "Why, even the theaters don't bring live talent to our pueblo; and the *evangelicos* provide us with a program like this—free!"

Our first borrowed tent was small, much patched, and mildewed. Later on we acquired a larger one. (The third tent seats fifteen hundred and can hold up to two thousand on a standing-room basis.) We still ran into active opposition from the enemies of the gospel, but it was harder for them to stop a tent meeting than one held in a public building. Another point recognized by civil authorities was that the drawings and special music had entertainment value; so that our program could not be condemned as "just a heretic preaching false doctrine."

For one campaign, the Lord had enabled us to secure a large parking lot in front of the central city plaza. On the second day, after a packed first night, a clerical dignitary came to inform us that our tent was erected on their church's property, and that we would have to take it down at once and move out of town. The campaign chairman, a fine Baptist pastor, faced him with no sign of annoyance and said softly, "Just bring us the title deed to this property, showing that it belongs to your church, and we will take the tent down." He knew, of course, that the lot belonged to the city. After a bit more bluster, the testy cleric gave up and left, but he was not done with us.

The next day a delegation of important religious personages and their lawyers went to call on the mayor. Their complaint, based on false rumors, described us as a "shouting, disorderly mob." They insisted that the mayor could not allow such meetings to continue in the very heart of the province's capital.

Unexpectedly, the mayor's secretary, a capable woman of middle years, stood up and said, "Mr. Mayor, this is not so. I have been attending the meetings each night. The people are quiet and orderly, the music is lovely, and the message is right from the Holy Bible."

We couldn't have had a better defense. The mayor decided that we could stay, and later on he gave us permission to stay several extra days so that we could close on a national holiday.

Since our meetings were open to all comers, they attracted some people who were used to loud exuberance in their own religious groups. So, on each opening night of a campaign, we warned such persons to be considerate and to avoid all shouting or unruly demonstration. One night, when I was about five minutes into my message, a man stood up and began to pray or speak in tongues in a loud voice. I pointed my finger at him, and in a tone of authority told him, "In the Name of Jesus, sit down and be quiet!"

It was like pricking a toy balloon. We heard no more from him, or from anyone else, from then on.

When we were campaigning in the Chaco region, at the edge

of the jungles, large delegations from Russian and German settlements came to swell our meetings, people who had emigrated from their native countries in search of religious and political liberty. The location of our tent was an ideal one, in the city of Roque Saenz Peña. To accommodate the masses from the town and outlying communities, we took off the sides of the tent. Borrowed planks made benches around the outside. For the entire week, two theaters in the city had to close down for lack of an audience. On our closing night, over thirty-five hundred people swarmed to the meeting. During the campaign, three hundred Bibles, two hundred and fifty Testaments, and many other books and leaflets were sold.

Afterward, Pastor Holowaty wrote to us: "Many new people are coming to the churches. At our church we don't know where to put them all. A hundred and sixty converts are faithfully attending and bringing their relatives."

Persons who, not many years ago, despised little isolated groups of evangelicals as being poor and ignorant, now treat them with respect. Not only has the evangelical movement produced Christ-filled lives among the humbler folk, but more and more business and professional people in Latin America have turned to the Lord.

10.

Of Death—And Life

I was preaching in Trenque Lauquen, eight hundred miles from home, when Evelyn, our youngest, was born. It would be ten days before I could see her!

When I did get there, surprise added to my thrill. "Evelina," as she is registered in the archives of Argentina, was a nearly perfect copy of our eldest, Ruth Ellyn, except that she was a very healthy little girl. The same eyes, the same silken blond hair! All her features, and much of her personality as it developed, were Ruth Ellyn's. (Evelina is now a long-legged, freckled girl of twelve, a keen student, gifted with rare artistic and musical talent.)

She was sent to bring us joy in the midst of deep affliction, for her "big" sister, our "pale, little flower," was soon to leave us. Moreover, the doctor was soon to tell us that Joey, one of the twins, could not live.

Joey's crisis came first, following a new onset of hepatitis. After six months in bed he had slipped out of the house to be with some of his chums—and had eaten some green apricots. They brought on a devastating attack of diarrhea. In the hospital I peered over the physician's shoulder at the fluoroscope and saw that the boy's liver was immense. His abdomen was swollen tight, and jaundice had turned his skin yellow, as yellow as if it had been painted. After the nurse had taken Joey out, the doctor said, "This child cannot possibly live."

Sick at heart, Ruth and I cried to God, and God answered. Through missionary friends, four precious glass capsules of a marvelous new liver concentrate were provided. This vital fluid, injected into a vein and followed by twenty more capsules, had much to do with starting our son's slow recovery. Though for long weeks the specialist offered us no hope, we continued fervently in prayer. By God's kind providence, my evangelistic meetings were in Cordoba, and I could relieve Ruth at Joey's hospital bed for part of every day.

At the same time Ruth Ellyn, now seventeen, was visibly failing. Most children with cystic fibrosis die at seven or eight years of age, but her life had been prolonged to bless us in answer to the prayers of hundreds, perhaps thousands, of God's people. Now the weakness and malformation with which she had been born were culminating in more and more distress. She needed constant nursing, which was no longer possible at home because of Joey's desperate illness, so we took her to a lovely sanitarium in the hills. There under the care of a Christian doctor, she seemed to be holding her own, and we hoped that she might come back home to be with the baby sister she so dearly loved.

Joey did come home, definitely and miraculously on the way back to health, so we were free from heart-wrenching anxiety, but not for long. One afternoon the sanitarium's station wagon stopped in front of our house, and the doctor came in to say that he was bringing Ruth Ellyn to the city "for tests." He suggested that her mother come along to the clinic.

Ruth found the child limp and pale, too weak to articulate her words clearly. At the clinic, Ruth turned her over to a nurse while she signed her in at the desk.

How could she possibly know that the nurse would lead our little invalid walking up two flights of stairs?

When Ruth found her, the child was feebly gasping for breath, barely conscious. After hours of waiting for expert attention, my wife decided that we must get our little girl out of that clinic and take her to the same large, well-equipped hospital that had so wonderfully cared for Joey. Ruth tried in vain to telephone me. Owing to Cordoba's tremendously rapid growth there was a scarcity of telephones in the city. The phone nearest our house was seven blocks away, and nobody answered it.

Desperate, my wife hurried to the public square where many buses pass, hoping to catch one for home, and there she found that a wildcat strike had stopped nearly all the buses! People were fighting for taxis. Ruth finally had to give up and walk back to the clinic, praying that I would sense that she needed help.

Unaware that there was any emergency, I telephoned the clinic later on, but I could get no answer. The office was closed for the night. And our car was laid up for repairs!

In the morning I did get a call through to Ruth, who had just been through one of the longest, darkest nights of her life. What she told me sent me racing out to the avenue. A bus passed with passengers hanging outside the doors. I grabbed a hold and hung on till we reached downtown Cordoba.

A few minutes later we were all in a police ambulance roaring through the streets to the big hospital where Ruth Ellyn was already well-known. Within moments after we arrived, our little sufferer was receiving the expert care she so desperately needed. The entire hospital staff was alerted. Doctors, specialists, technicians, all spontaneously offered help, along with the very latest technical equipment, to keep our daughter alive. They pored over her case history, made analyses, and studied X-ray pictures. They spared no effort which could possibly be of use.

Fortunately I could stay with Ruth at the hospital day and night, a boon which we gratefully received from the hand of the Lord. Ruth was by now in no condition to carry on alone.

Light and shadow were strangely mingled in our emotions as we watched our frail little girl's labored breathing. It seemed as if we ourselves were struggling along with her in an unending, desperate nightmare. The spasmodic, convulsive, stomach breathing continued through four days and nights, interrupted by strangled coughing spells that tore our hearts. We were able to recognize her mumbled words: "oxygen," "water," "nurse," and *"baño"*; but there were no complaints, no tears, no entreaties. She could not lie down. At times it was difficult for her even to rest at an angle against the pillows; and so for hours I held her precious head with its silken hair against my chest. A few moments of blessed sleep were for her like a gift from heaven, and the loud slamming of a door, or the roaring of a motorcycle engine in the street below assumed the proportions of a tragedy.

From time to time Ruth stretched out on the other bed, and I tried to catnap on a blanket on the floor; but sleep was next to impossible, and prayer was like breathing. Time after time, in the seventeen years past, sympathetic doctors had warned us that Ruth Ellyn could not survive the basic changes that would take place in her teens. Her tiny fingers with their clubbed nails, her racking cough, and other symptoms of long standing, all indicated that she was living on borrowed time; but nothing could have prepared us for these hours of agony. Nor for those moments, just after reaching the hospital, when the doctors could not find her pulse!

Once, after stepping into the hall for a minute, I returned to find Ruth trying with all her might to get Ruth Ellyn back into bed. In her delirium the child had decided to go to the bathroom. It was amazing what energy she displayed in this state, when she got the idea that she was in the wrong room, or that Mommy was upstairs and she must go to find her. Again and again she was at the point of dragging tubes, bottles, and all with her! At times she babbled about big spots on the walls, and once she saw bugs crawling over her mother's face and arms. Often she called out to assure herself that I was still there, and was much concerned that I was lying on the hard floor.

Our tears flowed silently as death moved closer and closer to our little one; and then—

On Saturday afternoon a change began—a change as distinct as day following night, and as gentle as the first soft breeze of spring after winter's bitter cold. Her Savior's Hand sweetly untied our little girl from everything of this sad world. He filled the room with a heavenly peace that took possession of Ruth Ellyn, and of us as well.

We had known, before that wonderful moment, that the Lord was near, standing in the shadows. We had been certain that all was in His blessed Hands. But now it was as if He had given a silent command to His holy angels: "From this moment, there must be no more suffering. Let the atmosphere of Heaven replace that of Earth."

I leaned close to our dear one and said, "Ruth Ellyn, *¿A donde vas vos?*" (Ruth Ellyn, where are you going?)

A smile of utter peace such as we had never seen lighted her delicate, almost transparent features, and slowly she turned her eyes toward me. In a murmur of supreme contentment she said, *"Al cielo."* (To heaven.)

"Y ¿Como lo sabes?" (And how do you know?)

Swift and sure as an arrow in flight came back her reply, *"Porque tengo a Cristo en mi corazón."* (Because I have Christ in my heart.)

No Christian parent could ask for more. Our anguish for all the sufferings of her lifetime seemed to melt away. For a number of years we had seen much evidence of a real conversion experience, but this was final and glorious confirmation. The nurses, accustomed to deathbed despair and bitter wailing, expressed their

deep amazement: *"Nunca hemos visto una fe tan maravillosa."*
(Never have we seen such marvelous faith.)

When she had entered the clinic, five days earlier, Ruth Ellyn
had told her mother, "Mommy, this is it"; and she had talked
about who should have her dresses and other clothes after she was
gone. Now we felt that she was already living with her Lord,
more in the other world than in this one. How precious were
those last hours alone with our unspeakably precious jewel! She
talked with joy of those she would see in heaven. She had been
studying in Sunday school about the great men of the Old Testament, so she began slowly listing those whom she would see:
"David, Solomon, Joshua, Esther . . . and Uncle Nate . . . and
Tío Arturo Hotton . . ." *

"And who will you see first of all, Ruth Ellyn?"

That heavenly smile lighted the whole room as she spoke His
blessed Name: "Jesus!"

I have often thought of Ruthie Ellyn as a delicate flower; and
while I usually called her "Beanie" aloud, my heart would say
with a certain sadness, "My pale, little flower!" There are hardy
flowers that grow in the sunbaked fields, sturdy of stem, with
coarse leaves and petals that open to the burning rays of the sun
without fear; but there are others that gently push their way up
through moist leaves that lie deep in the cool solitudes of the forest. There, protected by the strength of some overhanging crag,
they breathe forth their fragrant loveliness and shyly display their
delicate pastel colors.

Ruth Ellyn was just such a fragile flower, sheltered, hidden
away in the house much of the time, studying a little of her Cal-
vert home-study courses, playing so well on her violin, writing a
little in her diary in a clear, regular hand, attending the meetings

---

* Dr. Hotton was a wonderful Argentine friend who translated *Through Gates of Splen-
dor* into Spanish and wrote many beautiful hymns. He had been killed in an automobile
accident a few months before.

which were, fortunately for her, in our own living room. How she loved her new little sister, who brightened her last months on earth! How she enjoyed the tiny bunnies that scampered in and out of their burrow in their pen in the side yard!

How lovingly did the Savior pause in the woodland dell to gently disentangle the delicate root tendrils from the dank soil here, that our cherished flower might be transplanted to bloom in that celestial land where cool, crystal waters flow, and the gentle breezes caress those who shall never more know pain or sorrow!

Here in South America, where burials must take place within twenty-four hours, it was surprising to us how rapidly the word traveled. The night of Ruth Ellyn's departure, over a hundred Christian friends and neighbors came to the simple, moving service. There was much quiet weeping and many expressions of loving sympathy, even from those who had never before shown any particular interest in the "foreigners." Through death, God was touching hearts that could not otherwise be reached. If the birth of our Argentine baby had bound us closer to the people, the home-going of our eldest opened up deep fountains of love and affection.

At the funeral service, Daniel Ericsson brought a ringing message. He spoke of the immediate translation of a true believer into the glorious presence of the Lord. Francisco Bilbao sang two very beautiful songs, "The End of the Road," and one which is my favorite of all his solos, and which speaks of our eternal home, "Rejoice, O Happy Soul!"

I was afraid that my heart would be too full to let me speak at the service, but God, "Who only doeth wondrous things," gave Ruth and me special quietness, to bear testimony to His goodness and to the reality of our hope in Christ. We made clear that we "sorrow not even as others which have no hope." Rather, while we weep for the awful separation from our dear one, we know that "to depart and to be with Christ" is "far better."

It was characteristic of Ruth Ellyn that during her last hours she asked that we pray for an unsaved girl friend. Her earnest efforts to shine for Jesus, with her limited strength, will live on in our hearts, and they will give us lionlike courage in our battle to win men to Christ.

They did so on that same Saturday night, which saw the opening of a tent campaign in a very needy *barrio*. Although, right up to the time of the meeting, I felt weak and faint, the Lord infused my soul with superhuman power. As I drew the chalk picture of "heaven," my eyes were so blinded with tears that I could hardly see. Only the power of the Holy Spirit made it possible for me to preach. At the invitation, more than twenty came forward to accept the Savior. Among them was a lovely Argentine girl the same age as Ruth Ellyn. She said to herself, "If Jesus means so much to the evangelist that he would come here to preach the gospel to us while his daughter is dying, I must accept Him." She did, and today, ten years later, Nelida is a sweet Christian wife and mother.

It was all of God, all of God! He alone is worthy to receive honor and glory and might and dominion, both now and forever. Amen.

As we arrived at the cemetery, another group preceded us through the gates, wailing and shrieking hysterically. How unspeakably sad are the groanings and tortured cryings of lost sinners mourning for their loved ones who have died without hope!

11.

Rain, Mud, Wind, and Snow

For anyone who imagines missionary work to be a continual round of soul winning and glorious answers to prayer, I have a warning. Merely getting where one must go to preach can require heroic effort, especially in vast Argentina. Hardships and suffering are at times inescapable. We knew this, from our own experience before coming to South America, but new difficulties faced us here.

From the very start, transportation was a major problem, for we had no funds to buy a vehicle. We used the overcrowded buses, or else walked. Within a year we had a bicycle. Later, after much prayer, we were able to buy a microbus with a two cylinder motorcycle engine. This little "two-lunger" did fairly well in mud, with its front-wheel traction, but out on the broad pampas in a strong head wind it barely crawled along. Fine, abrasive dust worked its way into the wheel bearings, and of course when one of these burned out it had to be on a desolate dirt road fifty miles from nowhere.

Since the price of a good car or truck remained far beyond the limits of our budget, our next vehicle was also a "lemon." It was a badly constructed, buslike monstrosity—for one thing, the hand brake had never functioned—but it had more power and capacity than the microbus.

One day, approaching a narrow bridge, I drove up behind a

huge trailer truck. When I trod on the foot brake, it flopped loosely, disconnected somewhere below the floorboards. To avoid a fatal crash into the truck, I must either plunge into the river or pass to the left, straight into the path of a car that was already coming across the bridge.

I pushed the accelerator to the floor, and with a mental cry to heaven for help I shot past the truck. The oncoming car screeched, braking hard, as I swung back into the right lane with almost nothing to spare. The bridge was a long way behind me before I breathed freely again.

East of Cordoba, between Paraná and La Paz, there is today a wide, well-paved superhighway, but ten years ago this road was mud. One trip through it, slithering and sliding, trying to follow the deep ruts of a truck, cost us eighteen hours of heart-breaking toil. Five days of torrential rain had turned its sticky gumbo into a trap for anything on wheels. As we topped each little rise, I took a deep breath, got a firmer grip on the steering wheel, and prayed that we might keep going. When darkness forced us to stop, we tried to sleep, one of us on the front seat and the other on top of *bultos* of tent canvas. Local mosquitoes must have passed the word to distant swarms, for they all came to feast on us. When daylight broke, at long last, we had to dig great gobs of mud from the wheels before we could get started again.

At the halfway point, we found four big trailer trucks lined up where the drivers had been camping out for several days. When I asked about the road ahead, they shook their heads. *"Señor, es imposible seguir adelante."* (It is impossible to go on.) We tried it, however, and in a very short distance saw what the truckers meant. Before us stretched a kilometer of road completely under water.

We could never have driven through it, but there was a huge tractor on hand to help. This waddling monster hooked onto us with a cable and towed us, jerking and bucking, through the flood. Water rose to the floorboards, and I wondered if we were about to submerge. As it turned out, the water didn't get that deep, and we landed with our engine still usable. We slithered on through deep, wet ruts, reaching La Paz that night in time to put up our tent for the next day's evangelistic meeting.

On another rainy night of traveling I tried to sleep on the lumpy tent canvas in the truck—and failed. Then, something made me crawl to a side window and look back at the long, heavily loaded platform trailer—just in time to see a broken axle's end hit the pavement in a shower of sparks. The dual wheels hurtled off into the night. Our truck swayed dangerously, but Jim, a born *camionero,* wrestled it to a safe stop.

Haroldo, my tent caretaker, was able to switch wheels around, and for the next grueling five hundred miles to Bahia Blanca, his ingenuity kept them turning. In Azul, a God-sent mechanic, Manuel Martín, made changes in the springs and axle that solved our problem.

Another enemy of our tent campaigns was the wind—terrific wind that gathers strength in its long sweep over the *pampas.* Once, we had just got the tent up and stretched tight when I noticed a brown haze in the southeast. I knew what it meant, but there was no time to lower the tent. The windstorm struck like a cannonball. The tent went down with a *whoosh* in a tangle of ropes, stakes, and bent iron poles.

In another town, with our tent surrounded on three sides by two-story buildings, we thought we were safe; but the wind roaring overhead sucked the tent canvas up in flapping pieces and laid it over the rooftops.

Though blows like this seemed disastrous for the moment, we were usually able to sew the torn canvas and get the tent up for the next night's meeting. The great advantage of having two thousand people in a tent, as against two hundred in a building, more than justifies the risk of the wind. Although Satan has tried, time and again, to destroy our work, God has always intervened to prevent it.

Always, whether traveling in Alaska where snow squeaks underfoot in subzero cold, or island-hopping in the tropical Caribbean, or flying across the high Andes mountains, I have trusted a Heavenly Father to guard me. When I look out of a plane's window to see six-foot-long flames shooting from an engine, I do not really need the calm voice of the airline hostess to reassure me. I know that I am not at the mercy of men or chance, but can rest in the Hands of Almighty God.

Once while on a tour of the States, I was with Max Kent, a Christian film producer putting together a film for use in Spanish America. We were working around the clock, since I had to fly from Dayton, Ohio, to Philadelphia, for a meeting in my home church the following night. That winter night a big snowstorm hit the area blanketing the entire midwest. When I phoned the airline office the next morning, I was informed that due to the blizzard raging in Chicago, my plane flight had been cancelled.

Since my meeting was for that same night, it was now too late to get to my destination by ground transportation. What to do? I prayed, committing the matter to my Heavenly Father. In the meantime planes were stacked up over Chicago, going around in circles unable to land. Some were sent to Detroit, some to St. Louis. One was sent to Dayton. When the pilot asked for flight instructions, where do you suppose he was sent? To Philadelphia.

The girl phoned again. "How soon can you be out here?" she asked. "I'm practically there now," I fairly shouted, hanging up and grabbing my suitcase. Max lost no time getting to the airport, and in a few minutes I climbed aboard to face a difficult decision: There were eighty-five empty seats and I could not decide which one to sit in!

12.

Holding Forth
the Word of Life

"Precious in the sight of the Lord is the death of His saints" (Psa. 116:15). But how terrible can death appear to the unsaved!

One evening a group of poor neighbors, who lived just down the street from us, came to me for help. The old grandfather had come from his *rancho* to the city for an eye operation—and had dropped dead in the bathroom. Would I take the body back out to his home, they asked, along with those who wished to attend the funeral? An ambulance would be far too expensive for these very poor *peones*.

They put the dead man into our microbus, and as soon as we had started, began arguing how to smuggle the corpse past the police checkpoint without legal papers.

"Look here," I interrupted them. "I will not be a party to lies. I will speak with the police, and you will be quiet. God will help us."

At the checkpoint, when the policeman had noted my name and license number, I asked directions to the last town on our way to the open country. The officer was most polite. He became so absorbed in explaining, that he quite forgot to ask what, besides passengers, we were carrying.

"Adios, señor!" he called as we started on into the night.

132

We left the last little corner store and followed a dirt road through the fields. Away off, we saw a pinpoint of yellow light. After bumping along over some plowed ground, we came up to a low, dingy-white, adobe house. Gnarled old trees surrounded it, their tortured limbs reaching skyward like a mute plea for mercy.

I followed the corpse and its weeping bearers into a dimly lighted room. Distorted by kerosene lamp flames, their flickering shadows crept along the walls. They laid the body on the rough, unpainted dining-room table. A pitiful bouquet of wildflowers in a drinking tumbler had been placed nearby.

Slowly the room began filling up with relatives and neighbors —all deeply tanned, the older ones' skin wrinkled and furrowed by exposure—children of the soil. The shadowy room, the brooding faces, the grim corpse on the table, all were weird enough, but when the wailing for the dead began, I felt as though I had somehow crossed into an unknown world below the earth, peopled by gnomes. Pagan darkness surrounded me. There was a tarnished crucifix on the mud wall, and a faded, wrinkled print of the Blessed Virgin, but here all relation to Bible Christianity ended.

I wept silently with the family as the wake continued into the small hours of the night. I found opportunity to talk to one and another of the wonderful salvation purchased for us by a loving Savior's death on the Cross, but while each one to whom I spoke nodded assent, I knew that my words had little meaning for him. After doing what I could to show the love of Christ to those bereaved, I quietly paid my respects and left.

As I drove home alone, my heart cried out, "Oh, God! How terrible when death invades a family like this one! How awful to face the implacable enemy with no hope, with nothing but superstition and a few shreds of religion—without You, precious Lord, to take the darkness from their sorrow!"

Another call for help turned out very differently. Relatives of a woman who was dying without Christ asked me to go to the hospital and tell her how to be ready for eternity. The patient, they explained, was suffering from diabetes and complications. Barring a miracle, she could not live.

Accompanied by a member of our local church, I took a bus downtown. Reaching the small hospital, we climbed the stairs to the second floor. In the sickroom, a number of poorly dressed relatives stood at the foot of the bed, their eyes fixed on the ashen face of the *moribunda*. Fear showed in their dark eyes and drawn faces. They hardly noticed us.

A doctor entered briskly. He flashed a small pocketlight into the patient's eyes, felt for the pulse, pressed a thumb into the bloated flesh of her feet, and straightened up. Catching the eyes of the waiting relatives, he slowly shook his head. After he had left, a priest entered. He wore a dark, coarse, cowled robe, with a heavy crucifix on the chain around his waist, and in his hand was a small container of holy water. Murmuring Latin phrases through his full black beard, he sprinkled holy water over the bed, and went out. The impersonal rite seemed almost an affront to helpless grief. Where was the warm compassion these poor ones needed? Two thousand years ago, touched by others' sorrow, Jesus wept. *He* has not changed!

Standing against the wall with my brother in Christ, I thought to myself, "We have come too late!" But had we? Overwhelming sympathy for the sorrowing watchers gripped me. Faith began to grow, like water seeping into a dry well.

"Señores," I said gently, "you wouldn't mind if we prayed for your loved one, would you?"

"Oh, no, señor!" came the ready answer. "Of course you may do so."

As we knelt by the bed, our prayer rose from the depths of our hearts: "Oh, Father! Bring this woman back, that we may tell her how to be saved! Oh, God, nothing is too hard for You. Do it, Lord!"

Since my friend Miguel had to get up early the next morning to work, he took leave of the family and slipped out. Back against the wall, I stood silently watching, and waiting. Those at the foot of the bed stirred now and then, whispering among themselves. Time stood still. Ordinarily the grief-stricken relatives would have filed out after the rite of extreme unction, to make arrangements for the death wake; but now they waited.

I continued in prayer: "Oh, God, bring her back, even for a few moments!"

Suddenly I noted a very slight movement of the *moribunda's* upper lip over her toothless gums. She had started to breathe again. She kept on breathing. Her eyelids fluttered!

Within four days the "dead" woman was well enough to be taken to her daughter's house, just up the street from the hospital. Fortunately I was home between campaigns, and able to visit her each day. Seldom have I seen a heart more ready to receive the great Good News that Jesus saves. Her mind was lucid, as clear as the sunshine that streamed through her window to make a bright pattern on the floor. Her heart opened to the love of Christ like the mouth of a hungry nestling. Within three days she had thoroughly understood God's plan, and made her decision. The joy and peace that filled her could be felt by all who entered the room. Some months later she slipped quietly away to be with her Savior.

Doña María, although still young, had reached the bitter end of life. Her common-law husband had gone off, leaving her with three small children, whom she had tried to feed and clothe by whatever means she could. Each time she took a feeble step forward she slid two steps backward.

Maria had once been an attractive girl, cherished by her parents and sought after by young men. Now she was alone, so terribly alone! Because of her three small children, nobody wanted to hire her to work in a home. Maria had written to her brothers and other relatives, pleading for help, but they did not respond. No one came to her aid. She must put her pride in her pocket and beg for yesterday's bread at the bakery.

It did not occur to Maria to call out to God for help. She was a convinced atheist. When she was growing up, away out in the country, someone had given her a New Testament. Since even at that early age she despised all religion, Maria had passed the little book on to her mother—who read it, and was wonderfully converted. The mother tried in vain to get Maria to read the Bible, along with good Christian literature. Although the girl practically adored her mother for her sweet and gracious life, she insisted that she did not believe in God and that it would be a waste of time to read the Bible or any such "outmoded stuff."

Now, after long months with no relief in sight, Maria came to a grim decision: she must commit suicide. And into the tortured chaos of her mind came the most hideous thought of all: "I must kill my children, too. I can't leave them to suffer and be kicked around—to sleep in doorways and beg for crusts!"

But how would she do it? She had no gun and no money to buy one. Finally she thought up a simple plan. She would take them to a high precipice she knew of; then she would tie the children to her waist and jump off. They would all die together . . .

Sleepless, night after night, Maria watched the faces of her three innocents. They slumbered so sweetly, their features touched at times with the trace of a smile. Could she ever go through with her macabre plot? Yet, driven by daily hunger, the cold that penetrated her unheated shack, and the callous indifference of her neighbors, she saw no other way. Godless fatalism had so twisted her thinking that she felt sudden death would be best for her little ones . . .

It was Saturday night. Tomorrow, using the few pesos she had saved for this purpose, Maria would take her children on a bus that passed by the high precipice. Tomorrow they would leave this broken-down shanty forever. The piece of clothesline, frayed but adequate, was ready.

Sometime before dawn Maria sank exhausted into a chair, and in the darkness her mind harked back to better days that seemed so far away and unreal. One thing had been real—her mother's love. Her mother had died some years ago, but in her agony Maria cried out to the only person she had ever known to love her: "Dearest Mother, I am lost! I don't know which way to turn! Oh, Mother, *please* help me now!"

Worn out, she slumped down in the chair and fell asleep.

The first streaks of dawn were beginning to filter through the cracked, dusty windowpanes when Maria became aware of a stronger light that filled the room. There was her mother, looking straight at her, with unspeakable tenderness. Slowly, softly, the dear lips spoke: "My child, God never abandons those who belong to Him."

The vision faded and was gone. Maria sat for a while, overwhelmed. Then, sensing that something unknown, but of greatest importance, was going to happen this day, she commanded her tired body to get out of the chair. She combed her hair, struggled into her shabby coat, and went out, locking the door to keep her children from wandering into the street. She went first to a house where she had worked as a maid. They still owed her money. The lady of the house slammed the door in her face. Next she went to the bakery. The lady behind the counter, on hearing Maria's story, gave her several hard loaves left from the day before, and said, "My dear, God never abandons those who belong to Him."

Maria was startled. These were the very same words her *mother* had used!

Without knowing why, she made an unaccustomed turn as she left the bakeshop, and in doing so passed a small evangelical church. Urged by some inner force that she did not understand, she approached the bald, round-faced man at the church door. "Can anyone go in?" she asked.

The man smiled warmly. "Of course, señora! Everybody is welcome here." Then he explained that the meeting was just over; and with a friendliness that Maria hadn't encountered for a long time, he said, "Why don't you come back this afternoon? We are having a special speaker who will draw beautiful pictures and present the gospel."

Mumbling that she would return, Maria left him. That afternoon she was in the service, and in spite of her shabby coat she felt strangely at home. These people reminded her so much of her mother! The singing was so happy and wonderful. And there was prayer, prayer with a heart in it. These people not only believed that God existed; they spoke to Him as if they knew Him personally.

These prayers were followed by the chalk drawing, done rapidly in dramatic colors, of a jungle scene in Ecuador—a sandy beach and a demolished airplane, stark against a gloomy backdrop of tangled vines and giant trees. On the river, sharply silhouetted, a dugout canoe floated in a path of silvery light. While background music told of the love of God in song, the lights on the picture dimmed and brightened, gradually changing the colors. To Maria it all held an unearthly quality. She was deeply stirred.

Then came the message. The blond artist with the high forehead told about the brutal savagery of the Auca Indians. He told how they killed one another, and how they had murdered five brave young missionaries who had come to tell them of Jesus.

The five—one of whom was the artist's brother—came to that lonely beach knowing they might die; but they came with the message of God's Word, that Jesus could save even Auca Indians. He could take the hatred out of savage hearts and replace it with divine love.

The evangelist began talking of another kind of dying: dying to self and to sin, dying to the world in order to live a new life of peace and power—all because Jesus loved us enough to die for our sins on the Cross.

Maria was listening with all her soul. When the invitation was given to come forward and remain for prayer, she moved out into the aisle, like one in a dream. There, at the front, as she listened to the instructions and prayed to her mother's God, the burden of sin and hopelessness rolled from her heart. Her three little waifs had a new mother.

Soon her children were in an orphanage staffed by evangelicals, and Maria was a nurse in a hospital. Today she is healthy and well-nourished in spirit and in body. She attends church joyfully, and she is respected by all.

The outstanding feature of Doña Maria's new life was her great faith. She knew the God of miracles.

Once a young man was brought into the hospital from the country, dying of typhoid fever. After examining him, the doctors and nurses decided that he was past help. If he wasn't already dead, he soon would be. His blood pressure was almost zero.

Maria went to the grief-stricken father in the corridor. "You wouldn't mind if I prayed for your boy, would you?" she asked.

With his prompt consent, Maria went to his dying boy's side, placed her hands on him, prayed, and came out. At six o'clock the next morning—the time when the doctor had said the boy would die—his blood pressure was up and his pulse was strong.

In the meantime, Maria had led the father to Christ. He took the first bus back home to break the good news to his wife. She no sooner saw her son well on his way to recovery than she asked Maria to help her to be saved, too.

Maria's ministry was just beginning—a ministry which resulted from her attending a very humble meeting in a little church of some fifty believers.

Once, when the very man who had deserted her was thrown into jail without food or blankets, Maria brought him meals and covers—not because of any personal attachment, but because the love of Jesus was flowing through her to everybody in need, even to the man whose neglect had once pushed her to the brink of suicide.

13.

Miracles in the Jungle

From the start it was clear to me that itinerant evangelism could not possibly cover all of the towns and cities in South America that were crying for the gospel. Pictures drawn on my easel did attract large numbers of people, but I was limited to one meeting at a time, whereas by means of color films I could draw at many places at the same time—places I could never personally visit.

Actually, my first interest in "movies" dates back to some childhood experiments. While still in grammar school, I used to draw little stick figures on the bottom of each page of my notebook in a close sequence of action poses; then, by riffling the pages very fast, I made them seem to be running, jumping, falling, or gesturing.

Many years later, just before leaving for Japan, I had bought a little set-focus Keystone camera, with a few reels of film—all I could afford. As I went from place to place in that dramatic land, drawing and preaching, I tried to film every kind of scene that would help the folks "back home" visualize what the Pocket Testament League was doing, and the desperate need for that work. When I ran out of film, I picked up old reels here and there. Some of the results were pretty dark, and once I set the speed at sixteen frames per second, instead of thirty-two. Of course this made the subjects seem to dash about like crazy people!

As fast as I used up my film, I mailed it back to Max Kent in Dayton, Ohio. Max had commanded a crew of thirty or so at the air base there, making technical and educational films for training servicemen. So, if he said the film I sent was "usable," I took it for high praise. If once in a long while he called it "very good," this meant the footage was fantastically beautiful or poignant. Our friendship fed and grew upon our mutual desire to spread the gospel, especially on the foreign mission field. Lack of funds for our projects troubled both of us, but Max stood ready to make any sacrifice he could.

I must have tried the patience of my PTL teammates sorely. It was nearly impossible to obtain proper lighting at that time in Japan. I struggled with what I had. My friends never knew when I would stop the truck and race to some vantage point to shoot footage. But in the end we produced three Japanese films, which helped a great many "home folks" to see the vital work PTL was doing in the Far East.

I nearly missed my chance to film the Auca Indians of Ecuador—a truly startling subject, and my first South American motion picture. On my way to visit Rachel, who had been working for a long time and with God's great blessing to evangelize these jungle killers, I stopped in Lima, Peru. There, at the airport store, I saw some reels of film and debated whether or not to buy them. I didn't know if Rachel would permit me to use them among her still very primitive Indians. Totally unacquainted with civilization's ways, they might be alarmed or offended by the camera's searching "eye." On a chance, I bought half-a-dozen reels of black-and-white film.

Shortly afterward, I found myself in a helioplane—a marvel of jungle aircraft—circling the small clearing where Rachel was living with the Aucas. We touched down, and as soon as we had rolled to a stop the Indians surrounded us, all of them talking excitedly. Rachel, in the midst of this carrousel of brown skin, loud sport shirts, and makeshift skirts, seemed imperturbably herself, and quite at home. A second look at the Auca faces gave me something of a start, especially the sight of their large perforated and stretched earlobes, which flapped as their owners moved about. Among the older ones, some teeth were missing, but their broad smiles were warm and reassuring.

Soon I was seated at the table, watching Rachel prepare food. Before it was ready, an Indian elbowed his way through the intensely curious crowd, carrying a bowl of what looked, at first glance, like curdled milk. From descriptions I had heard, I recognized *chicha*. Worse still, I knew how it had been made—by women sitting in a circle, chewing starchy roots and spitting the product into a pot! Enzymes in the saliva had started the "ripening" and improved (for savages) the flavor of the unfermented mess.

With evident pride the Indian cupbearer placed the bowl down in front of me and stepped back, so that all the village could watch me drink the beverage especially prepared for their honored guest, brother of their missionary. I knew I was in deep trouble. To drink or not to drink? One horn of the dilemma pointed straight at my stomach; and the other one—?

Trying to keep my desperation from showing, I asked my sister (in English or Spanish, I don't remember which), "Sis, do I have to drink this awful stuff?"

"They'll be offended if you don't," she said in her matter-of-fact way.

I sent up an S.O.S. to heaven: "Lord, if You ever helped a poor missionary, help me now!"

In an act of faith, I downed it all, in two or three gulps. The

Indians were delighted, and went rushing off looking for a second bowl. Now, I don't like to be selfish about anything, so when it came I generously gave it to my sister.

That was my initiation. I was soon learning much about Rachel's work. I shot footage whenever enough light filtered through the dense rain forest to make filming possible. I learned that these Indians are used to the semigloom of the jungles and are almost never in full sunlight except when poling their canoes, out on the river. I am sure they had no idea of what I was doing, hiding behind my little black box while a "bumblebee" buzzed inside it. However, they did what Rachel and Dayuma told them to, and were wildly delighted with the Polaroid photos of themselves I took and showed just moments afterward.

I had heard outsiders express doubts that any of the Aucas had experienced genuine salvation. Granted, they said, that these Indians smiled and laughed a lot, but who could tell what they really felt and thought? Savages who never heard the gospel have been known to smile and laugh—and then commit murder the next minute!

I wish such doubters could have been with me among these Indians. Rachel and Dayuma recounted incident after incident which proved the Aucas' living faith. Dayuma herself was the best proof of all.

Once Dayuma, who loved Rachel with unsurpassed devotion, looked up from the campfire they had built and said earnestly, "Star,* if the downriver Indians come out of the jungle to attack us, I am going to stay by your side and die with you."

Rachel thought for a moment, then replied, "No, Dayuma. If they come I cannot escape, but you can; and you must do so in order to continue teaching your people about Jesus."

I got acquainted with Kimu and his wife Dawa. When Rachel,

---

* *The name the Aucas gave Rachel.*

Betty Elliot, little Valerie, and Dayuma first came into the jungle, this savage couple forgot all about eating and sleeping. They just wanted to hear, over and over again, the wonderful story of God's salvation. They were the first ones, after Dayuma, to be saved. All their lives they had lived in fear of evil spirits and evil men. Now they were unafraid, because they knew that Jesus had more power than all of the forest devils put together; and if other savages should kill them, they would surely go to heaven, where nobody kills anybody.

I saw a photograph of Dayuma, taken by Rachel when Dayuma was a poor pagan woman who had fled from the tribe during a massacre. She had found employment in a *patron's* cane fields and was working like a slave. When I put this chance snapshot side by side with a recent photograph of Dayuma, now the native missionary to her own tribe, the contrast was incredible. It was not "civilization," but Christ, who had changed her life.

(The same thing is true of Kimu and Dawa. Rachel has a motion picture film of Kimu working on a blowgun dart, before he came to Christ. A film of him and his lovely wife, several years after their conversion shows the contrast. The hard lines of fear and hate which stamped the old face are gone forever.*

I baptized nine converts at the Auca village of Tiwaeno. The Indian who helped me was one of those who had speared to death my brother Nate, and the last of the Indians baptized was another of the five living killers. He went under the baptismal waters in my grasp, now my brother in Christ!

Rachel herself is a walking wonder, a miracle of God's grace. I saw her day after day, busy with the primitive demands of jungle living, serving as teacher, nurse, and spiritual mentor, and obviously happy in it all. I marveled again at what Christ can do with a life wholly yielded to Him.

---

* On February 22, 1971, Kimu and Dawa appeared on the NBC television show, "Today," with Rachel and Gikita. The three Aucas, with my sister, were appearing at a number of rallies in the United States in behalf of the Wycliffe Bible Translators.

Rachel's thatched hut impressed me with its sound construction, but I was a bit surprised that it was screened all around. "Rach," I asked her, "do you really need all this screening? You have more bugs inside the hut than outside!"

She smiled at my ignorance. "The screens aren't for bugs," she told me. "They are to keep out the vampire bats that come at night and suck the blood of sleeping victims."

Speaking of bugs—the Aucas have something far better than flyswatters. It is a tiny monkey who moves so fast that I couldn't possibly film one in action. No larger than your fist, he moves with lightning rapidity, darting here and there, even up into the rafters, cleaning out the moths and the bugs in a very short time. But more always come in.

Watching my sister, so at home in a savage jungle, I recalled the time when, still a teenager, Rachel was taken under the wing of wealthy and cultured Mrs. Parmelee. That dowager's special fondness for Rachel made her envision the girl's acceptance in her own millionaire circle. She had taken Rachel abroad, sailing first-class on a great ocean liner, and staying at a famous luxury hotel in England. There, observing how the idle rich lived—an existence alien to the deep spirituality of her parents—Rachel grew more and more uncomfortable.

On their return trip she made her decision. As the great liner *Aquitania* was nearing New York Harbor, Rachel went out on deck early in the morning to look for the Statue of Liberty. Standing there under the vast, calm dome of God's sky, she told Him she would never be satisfied until her life was wholly His.

"Right after that," she later recalled, "we all started going to Percy Crawford's evening Bible school. From there I went on to the Philadelphia College of Bible, then to Keswick, then to missionary training, and finally to Peru with the Wycliffe Bible Translators."

Rachel's commitment to work for the Lord, and for Him only,

deeply offended imperious Mrs. Parmelee. She cut Rachel out of her will, leaving her the smallest token she could think of—a pair of French miniature cuff links. At the time of Mrs. Parmelee's death, my sister was working in the office of the Keswick Bible Conference Center. The office burned to the ground, and Rachel lost most of her clothes in the fire, leaving her only one shirtwaist, which was made to be worn with cuff links. But Rachel had no cuff links and no money to buy any. Then came Mrs. Parmelee's legacy—and her only shirtwaist could be worn. So God plans our lives, down to the smallest detail!

The office fire seemed to have ended Rachel's usefulness at Keswick, and to signal God's readiness for her to enter on the work that she had always longed to do. When she was younger, she had been turned down by the China Inland Mission, for a back condition that God has since taken care of. Through the pain of her disappointment, she had felt her missionary vocation as strongly as ever, and along with it God's command: "Wait, till I call." The call had finally come, and Rachel wound up completing the work our brother Nate died to begin.

At Tiwaeno, trying to capture the story of the Aucas on celluloid for the outside world, I looked for details that would best point up how they lived.

One afternoon, when I and a dozen Aucas were refreshing ourselves in the Tiwaeno River close to the village, my companions suddenly yelled and scattered. I didn't know what it was all about, but I raced for the bank along with the rest. Safe on dry land, they told me that a water boa had appeared.

Another day, I found myself in a canoe which my bronzed and powerfully muscled Auca companions were poling along the river. Strange birdcalls floated to us through the dim, all-enveloping forest. The trees on both banks were taller than any others I had ever seen. Draped with hanging vines, they were majestic, reaching up and up for the sun. I couldn't escape the suggestion of organ pipes and the soaring arches of a vast cathedral. This was Ecuador's now famous Curaray River, at the moment silent, tree-shadowed, inscrutable; farther on, it would become a furious current, and the sun would be blazing down on us with furnace heat. I wondered how the Auca crew could manage our narrow, tippy craft in swift, rock-studded water.

I wondered more when we were swept into its treacherous crosscurrents. Again and again it seemed as if our dugout canoes must capsize; but all of them came through safely, thanks to superb boatmanship, and I looked with new respect at my jungle guides.

They were great boatmen, but their true grandeur was of the spirit. When they became Christians—these former killers and their fear-haunted women—they had counted the cost. Their stand for Christ might call for martyrdom any day, any hour; and they were ready. Even at this moment other Indians could appear on the riverbank, surround and slaughter us, as mercilessly as they had speared my brother Nate and his four dedicated friends. My Auca companions would not lift a spear in their own defense. Ambassadors of the King of Love, they could not "return evil for evil."

I glanced at Giketa, the leader of that bloody spearing party in 1956. He was older now, wearing the remnant of a visored cap that Rachel had given him. The visor had long since disappeared, but he still wore the cap like a badge of honor, the gift of "Star." Except for the difference that Jesus Christ had made in his face and manner, he still looked the jungle savage. The canoe pole in his strong hands might have been a twelve-foot-long *chonta* spear.

Fear and hatred had dominated the world into which he'd been born. Murder and cruelty were its natural expressions. The last frantic desire of a speared or disabled man was to be buried alive, since this alone could assure him that his body would not be eaten by worms. If a newborn child was thought too thin or too weak, it was thrown out into the bushes for the forest predators. A favorite amusement in the old days was brushing a branch of stinging nettles over the naked bodies of children, and roaring with laughter at their screams of pain. Giketa's village group had been facing extinction within ten or twenty years, by warfare and interfamily murder, when the gospel changed everything.

Giketa's people were taking me downriver to "Palm Beach," where my brother Nate and his four fellow martyrs were buried. The trip would take almost two days. We were traveling with the current, which was difficult and dangerous enough. The return trip, upstream, would be doubly hard.

At midday we stopped, while the women got out of their dugouts and waded in to the bank. As they walked, they lifted rocks and pounced on whatever had been hiding underneath. This assortment of jungle fish and other crawling things was thrown into the canoes, and would later enrich the common cooking pot. Back at Tiwaeno I had eaten some things that were far from appetizing; but Dayuma had graciously brought along more palatable food for me on this trip.

Dayuma was the only Indian with whom I could communicate, other than by smiles and gestures. She spoke Spanish and Quechua as well as her native Auca tongue. The others spoke only Auca; and when my face failed to register understanding, they spoke louder, feeling that somehow this would help me get their meaning. After all, what they were saying was perfectly clear to *them!*

The trip was fatiguing, despite the thrill of ever-changing river vistas. At times we had to get out and haul the canoe over a fallen giant tree, or past a shallow stretch of white water. When at last the evening shadows lengthened and the weird croaking of tropical frogs began, I became more acutely aware of how far I was from my civilized world—or even from Tiwaeno Village where Sis was living.

Finally our canoes were beached for the night. After some animated conversation, my Auca companions scattered in several directions, each one to his assigned task. One man vanished like a puma into the matted underbrush, and a moment later was scaling a tall species of palm tree. Near the top, he cut down a large bunch of nuts. Two men quickly unwound their fishing lines, and another pair began cutting down palm fronds. When they had enough, they wove them expertly into thatch for several simple lean-to shelters.

The women started a fire for cooking. We heard the report of the shotgun, and in a few minutes our Auca hunter returned with a black, long-necked, jungle turkey. Tough or not, it was a real prize. Aucas are most careful not to miss with the gun, since each hard-to-get shell is as precious as a gold nugget.

After supper, bone-weary, I crawled into my small, triangular, thatched *choza*. In deference to my civilized weaknesses, it was furnished with a rubber air mattress and a mosquito net.

Suddenly it was morning. The camp was abandoned, and we were again on our way to the tragic beach now familiar to millions of people through photographs in *Life Magazine* and the *Reader's Digest*. The beach's contour had been much changed since that day, by the fury of many floods; but the Indians knew exactly where the grave of the five martyrs was.

When we landed and I stepped out of the dugout, my feelings were indescribable. Walking over the coarse sand to the stump of the tree which had once supported the missionaries' tree house, I felt almost as if Nate himself were speaking to me. I visualized the killers' maddened faces and the savage violence with which they cast their spears. Again I saw five lifeless bodies thrown into the river—some with broken spears still hanging from them.

Then I recalled what Giketa had told Sis: "Oh, Star, then my heart was full of hate, but *now* it is healed!" I remembered the words of Dawa, who helped the murderers. "Dying," she said, "we shall see these white brothers again, and seeing them we shall be happy." And somehow my own troubled thoughts were healed.

We moved a few meters into the heavy underbrush, and stopped at a sunken area. The Indians stood silent, taking in each small detail. Then Dayuma said something in a low voice, and Giketa stepped forward to plant a slender bamboo cross at the head of the grave. We all bowed our heads as Dayuma prayed. The presence of God was very real here in the jungle gloom, more real than the pitiful remains lying a few feet underground.

The startling silence of the jungle returned, and I realized that Dayuma's prayer had ended. The Indians looked up, and we filed back onto the sand and into the sunshine. What I felt now was a buoyant, joyous sense of victory. Victory through "our Savior Jesus Christ, who hath abolished death, and hath brought life and immortality to light through the gospel" (II Tim. 1:10). Hallelujah!

The long, hard, return trip upstream was anticlimactic. At the landing, some little distance from Tiwaeno Village, we left the canoes drawn up on the beach, and the Indians plunged into a dark jungle trail. Suddenly rain began to fall in drenching, stifling sheets. I had on old sneakers, and their smooth, worn soles slipped on the wet leaves and skidded in the slippery mud. The Indians' strong feet and toes, shod only with leather-hard callouses, easily gripped the soil. They flew on ahead of me, their one thought being to reach the comfort of their huts before nightfall. I struggled along behind them, my heart pounding furiously, as I slipped and staggered. I slid down into little ravines and clawed my way up out of them. I scrambled over the rotting trunks of fallen trees, wondering how long my middle-aged heart would take the strain.

Through the gloom, far ahead, I saw the Aucas crossing a tremendous tree which had fallen across a deep gulch, moving like circus acrobats over its slippery length, and disappearing into the green twilight. All except Giketa. As he reached the far end of the trunk, he stopped, looked back, and came quickly to my aid. When I got there, panting like a dog, Giketa grasped my hand; and in that powerful grip I lost all fear of slipping off the wet, slick log into the gully below. Loving concern flowed out from a redeemed savage heart to mine. It was a symbol of what the grace of Jesus Christ can do, around the world, wherever hearts are opened to Him.

14.

Black Clouds over Tiwaens

There are many non-Christians, I suspect, whose mental picture of the savage is that of a happy, uninhibited child of nature in a sort of tropical paradise. They imagine him as a simple soul who enjoys his own quaint religion and is better off without a Christian missionary.

People who have had actual, daily contact with savages anywhere in the world know that such a picture is pure fantasy. Pagan tribesmen are anything but happy. Their life is a losing battle with "devils," with vengeful human enemies, and with brutal hardships. They are in constant terror of death. No one but Christ can win that kind of war; and His missionaries must lead the assault, as Rachel has done in Auca Land.

The wise missionary, of course, does not try to impose the patterns of "western" civilization on a savage community. He is not sent to change savage styles of housing or clothing or cooking. His work is to convince the pagan that God in love redeemed him and that Christ's power can transform him.

During my brief stay with Rachel, the situation of the Christian Aucas was relatively stable, but after my departure, black clouds of trouble gathered around Tiwaeno. On three sides, the white man, hated by the pagan Aucas, was closing in with his firearms and his strange oil rigs. Bloodshed had occurred in the past and much more was likely. This meant that time was running out for Rachel and the converted Indians to reach their pagan neighbors for Christ before guerrilla war should break out against the oil-company crews. Without God's help, Tiwaeno's outreach to the fierce, suspicious killers from downriver would be a hopeless gesture as well as a dangerous one. Yet these Auca missionaries, former killers themselves, knew that "God specializes in things thought impossible." With Rachel, they would go ahead, after dealing with a more immediate problem—the growing boldness of certain young rebels within the Tiwaeno group.

These hotbloods were still murderers at heart, very much so! Though they had seen their parents' lives transformed by Christ, they had reverted to the old tribal pattern. At meeting time in the village they would gallop past the "God's-speaking-house," shouting nasty remarks to distract the worshipers. There was even talk among them of killing Rachel.

Rachel's response was more prayer, and more prompt, fearless action. She went to the hut of one young rebel after another, rebuked him sternly but with motherly love, and confiscated the spears that had been made for murder. These fearsome weapons she hid under her own bed. She saved the lives of many men and women, for the age-old killing pattern spared neither sex. In all the Auca groups Rachel had made contact with, only one woman that she knew of had survived intertribal and interfamily murders to pass the age of fifty.

In the midst of this explosive situation, Tiwaeno was struck with an epidemic of poliomyelitis. Thirteen victims died, some quickly, others with agonizing slowness. Three pulled through with the help of a portable iron lung and therapy. Rocking devices were made, hand-operated, to force a little air into paralyzed chests. Rachel herself came down with the disease, but in a comparatively mild form; and she was able to carry on through the terrible, six-months' siege.

At first Rachel and the Christian Indians were blamed for the epidemic. Tempers flared. Paganism, like a chained giant, threatened to break its shackles and take control. Men who had lost wives began planning to kill some other men and take their widows. One man, Tidonca, began furiously making a spear when he saw that his son, a fifteen-year-old Christian youth, must surely die—a spear with which to vent his grief and frustration in murdering his daughter. The boy, with his last strength, pleaded, "Father, don't cry the way you do in the tribe. I am going up to God in heaven."

When death came, the parents bound their son's corpse with vines, knees drawn up to the chest as is the custom. The distraught father tucked his finest, rarest feathers between the boy's knees and chest. The mother shouldered the body alone and carried it out for burial. As the desperate man watched her, calling out, "My son! Oh, my son!" Rachel picked up his spear and started to leave by the back of the hut. A scream halted her.

"Star! Don't take my spear! Don't take it!"

"Tarendi," Rachel answered quietly, "you said you would not kill. I am helping you to keep your word."

This spear joined the others under Rachel's bed.

One of those whom the pagan Indians blamed for the polio deaths was old Parrot, a former witch doctor. He had murdered a number of people before coming under the influence of the gospel. Polio had stricken him, too; but now the young rebels of the tribe were talking of killing him, and thus ending the curse.

Parrot was not living in the village, but in another clearing. At Dayuma's request, Rachel had Parrot brought to Tiwaeno by a back way, and had his hammock slung under her own hut, for what protection this might give him. His would-be killers fol-

lowed him, as might have been expected; and, lying there helpless, he could hear them planning his death. However, Rachel's
outspoken logic held them back.

"Why, you crazy people!" she said to them. "What witch doctor would put the same curse on himself and his family, along
with the rest of the people this plague has struck down?"

Adding to all the tension, news came that a large group of
pagan Aucas from downriver were soon to arrive, curious to hear
about the true God Who taught people how to "live well." These
Indians were coming in response to friendship flights that the
missionary plane had made over their clearings. Communication
from plane to ground had been made by means of the "electronic
basket" lowered on a rope as the plane flew in a tight circle. With
this device the Auca "missionary" in the plane could converse
with potential murderers and be safe from their spears.

In view of the dangerous rebellion that certain village youths
were fomenting, the Lord inspired Sis to invite our brother Ben
for a brief visit to Tiwaeno before the hundred-strong group from
downriver should appear. One look at Ben, who stands six feet
three inches in his socks and weighs nearly two hundred pounds,
should put something like awe in the hearts of Tiwaeno's young
troublemakers; for the Auca men are short of stature. In their
minds, it would somewhat make up for Rachel's cultural disad-
vantage in being "just a woman." Ben's visit should also be a spiritual encouragement to the Christian Aucas, for Ben is a Baptist
pastor, with a passion for souls and a special interest in the Aucas.

Rachel's message to Ben told him that he must come right
away or not at all, since for him to be at Tiwaeno after the downriver group had appeared would be extremely dangerous. Ben
agreed to come, but funds for the trip were not immediately
available. He did have the film, *I Saw Aucas Pray,* which Max
Kent and I had shot in the jungle and Max had produced. Ben
showed this film in a number of churches that he could reach

quickly, and soon he had his passage money. Even so, a fast trip looked impossible, because it was summer, and the airlines were jammed with tourist traffic.

Miraculously, he met with no delays. In Quito, Ecuador, he saw a missionary and asked for Don Johnson, who is at the head of the Wycliffe Translators in that country. Don was at the airport. He rushed Ben through customs and got him aboard a mission plane which was leaving for the jungles at that very moment.

Ben could stay at Tiwaeno for only two days, but that gave him time enough to conduct meetings by interpretation, hold a baptismal service in the river, and celebrate the Lord's Supper. Rachel told him that she was most anxious for the Indians to understand the serious offense of eating and drinking at the Lord's Table unworthily; so Ben emphasized this solemn truth. He said that because of unconfessed sin in their lives, while partaking of the elements, some become "sickly" and some "sleep," that is, die. Spoken by a big man like Ben, these words carried a lot of weight.

Among the first Aucas to testify in this meeting was young Iniwa. He was the one about whom Stevie, Nate's son, had been so concerned. Iniwa had been given away by his mother, following a tribal custom. When young Stevie heard of it, he was horrified. He could hardly believe that any mother would willingly give away her own little boy. But Iniwa was now a young man; and at the Lord's Supper he confessed that he had talked of killing Rachel and other Christians. He vowed that he would talk that way no more. All who heard him were much impressed to hear this youth declare his repentance when partaking of the Lord's Supper.

The impression was sadly marred, not long afterward, when word came by portable transceiver from Dayuma, downriver, that Iniwa had come to that area and had killed old Parrot's son, along with a couple of younger children of the now converted

Palm Beach killers. Those men who speared the five white missionaries in 1956 have been firm Christians since their conversion,
ready to die rather than take life. However, there remained the
possibility of revenge by other relatives of Iniwa's victims, as
Dayuma was well aware. She guarded Iniwa day and night, not
letting him out of her sight. She hardly slept for days, in order to
protect the other children who were with her in the clearing
where she was harvesting her small crop of manioc. When Iniwa
did slip off into the jungle, Minkaye, a Christian man, went after
him, took one of his spears, and broke it up. Then Dayuma called
for the mission plane to fly overhead, so that Iniwa would realize
that his brutal crime was known at Tiwaeno.

One evening, about ten days later, Iniwa reappeared at Tiwaeno; while playing on the river beach with others, he fell down
in a faint. His companions were somewhat alarmed but Iniwa got
up laughing and said, "Oh, it is nothing."

A few minutes later he collapsed again, almost at Dayuma's
feet, in a terrific fit. His writhing and screaming were so hideous
that Sammy, Dayuma's son, climbed into bed and covered his
head. Iniwa foamed at the mouth, stiffened, and died.

A careful examination of the body showed no sign of poisoning
or of disease or of physical injury. Rachel firmly believes that
Iniwa was judged for his sin in giving false testimony at the
Lord's Table. Like Ananias and Sapphira in the days of the apostles, he had lied to the Holy Spirit when he made a false profession of faith. Like them he died and was carried out of the community. With great sorrow the Christian Aucas buried him at
Palm Beach, where he had been baptized and where my brother
Nate's body lies with his martyred companions.

But what a difference! Instead of dying for God, Iniwa died for
his wickedness. Doubtless he was not the only young Auca who
had made a false profession of conversion; but since all knew the

circumstances of it, his death was surely a warning that "God is not mocked" with impunity.

Gomoki was an Auca girl whom Rachel had brought out of Quito, where she had lived as a household servant and worse for eighteen years after fleeing from her tribe. While in Quito, she had acquired a thin veneer of Catholicism; and one day at Tiwaeno she said to Dayuma, "You have no god in your church."

Dayuma replied, "If you mean those objects made by man, which fall and break in a million pieces—why, no, we don't. But we have the true and living God."

During the polio epidemic, this poor girl had come over to Rachel's hut to scold the missionary for "ordaining" that her brother be killed by the dread disease. Rachel said to her, "Gomoki, you know that I came here as a servant of God. I didn't ordain such a tragic thing. I am just as sorry as you are, and more so."

Gomoki's temper simmered down at that response; and after a moment of thought the girl said, "I hear that your mother has died."

"Yes, Gomoki," my sister answered, "and she loved you very much. She wants to see you in heaven. But you will never see her there unless you ask God to cleanse your heart."

Rachel pressed her point: "What if you should die in one day, like your sister, with this polio? What would happen to you?"

Gomoki was edging out of the hut, but before she ran off Rachel had one last word for her: "If you don't ask God to cleanse your heart, you'll go down the devil's trail to the devil's house, and you'll never see my mother, because there's a great gulf fixed between."

Within twenty-four hours Gomoki was dead, not of polio, but of a jungle spearing. Another young Indian, raised in a Christian environment at the village, had married a downriver heathen girl. She put pressure on him to avenge the loss of his two younger brothers, according to the age-old Auca rule: "Lose a brother, kill a sister." (It doesn't matter whether the "sister" had anything to do with the brother's killing or not.) So this young husband killed Gomoki.

The large group of downriver Indians arrived, in a fever-ridden condition, fortunately, too weak to start any spearing. Thus Rachel and the converted Aucas had a little time both to tell and to show them the blessings of peace. The "impossible" task of evangelizing these potential enemies was at least under way. They were still suspicious and utterly unpredictable, and in the blackness of the jungle night their weird, spine-chilling chants rose endlessly, to placate or to ward off forest demons. In their fear of these evil spirits the Indians are capable of any extreme; and yet—

Not long ago, word came through that there were over two hundred Aucas living peaceably together at Tiwaeno, and that a still larger group of pagan Indians is yet to be reached in a different sector of the jungle. The song that the five martyrs sang before their tragic, final encounter with the Aucas on Palm Beach still strikes the keynote for God's messengers:

> *"We rest on Thee, our Shield and our Defender;*
> *Thine is the battle, Thine shall be the praise.*
> *When passing through the gates of pearly splendor,*
> *Victors, we rest with Thee through endless days."*

In a lighter mood, I often recall the day when I renewed my acquaintance with Rachel's Indians in the states. It was a few years ago, when Rachel was on her way to the worldwide conference on evangelism in Berlin. She arrived at the home of the Ad-

cocks in Huntingdon Valley, Pennsylvania, our family's home-
town. She had two Aucas in tow. I happened to be there, at the
same time.

The Indians looked very different from the jungle dwellers I
remembered. They were now wearing business suits, heavy over-
coats, and felt hats. And what boots! They were enormous, and I
guessed why. Since Kimu and Kome had never worn shoes before, their toes were splayed out like fans. Such feet would never
fit in a regular, pointed shoe.

The two smiled broadly as they greeted me, peering out from
under their hat brims, and I smiled back—our only means of
communication. But not long afterward Rachel came up to me,
brisk and businesslike, and said that she had to go to the dentist.
She added that the two Indians needed a good bath, and I was
hereby delegated to give it to them. Just like that!

"Look, Sis," I pleaded, "the only word of Auca that I know is
Waodani, the name they call themselves, so I can't possibly give
this pair a bath."

"You won't have any trouble," she replied easily. "Just use the
universal language. Just act out what you want them to do."
With that, she hurried out.

I looked my charges over. Since they both looked alike to me it
didn't matter which would be first in the tub. I smiled at one. He
grinned back at me. "You must now take a bath—" I started to
say and realized it would be a waste of breath. I gently prodded
him—it was Kimu—toward the bathroom. Since his hat and coat
were off, I at least had a start.

I turned on the water, and Kimu was instantly entranced. I
guess he thought the wall was full of water, and that one just
stuck a pipe in anywhere and out it came. I made signs to indicate
that he should take off his clothes. Kimu understood what I
wanted, but he didn't comply; he didn't see the point. When it
rains in the jungle, Aucas just wear their scanty clothing until it

dries. Very simple! But it only complicated my present problem. Finally, with some more pantomime antics, I succeeded in getting Kimu's outer clothing off. That was all.

Into the water he got, and I decided to get on with the job, regardless of the underwear. I started working with soap and a washcloth on his broad back and massive chest, and in the process managed to slip off his undershirt.

After both of them had been scrubbed, I got them into dry clothing, and then realized that there was one more chore to take care of. Sis had mentioned earlier that, since the Aucas run all day and every day in the jungle, it was essential that they get daily exercise on this trip. Of course, I was the one who must take them for a walk.

So out we went, *clump, clump, clump!* I put an arm around each of them and gently propelled them out to the country road that was actually a private lane. They smiled widely, and off we went, with their perforated, stretched earlobes dangling loosely below the crammed-down hats. We had started three abreast, but the Aucas promptly dropped behind me, to follow in single file, the only way people ever traveled in the jungle. If ever in my life I felt silly, it was then, tramping along that Huntingdon Valley lane ahead of two chunky Indians. I glanced at the houses along the way to see if people were watching. They were. I imagine the neighbors enjoyed our little procession as much as the Aucas enjoyed seeing the squirrels and the unfamiliar birds in the trees.

We brought Mother up to the Adcocks' home to see the film, *I Saw Aucas Pray*. Since we had planned to show it to the Indians, we thought that K-Ma would enjoy watching it with them. She knew all of the Aucas by their names and photographs, and she had prayed earnestly for them every day for years. Mother was now a thin, much wrinkled old lady but her smile lighted up the whole room wherever she was. She had lost nothing of her "pert and chipper" manner; we guessed that her series of health-food diets had proved their worth for her, at over eighty years of age.

K-Ma greeted each one of us brightly, paying special attention to the two swarthy Indians, and then we all sat down to see the film. I don't think Mother looked at the screen at all. She was observing the reactions of Kimu and Komi the whole time. Those two watched the entire film with rapt attention. When their own village with its assorted people and animals appeared, they chattered like magpies and went off into gales of laughter, pointing out first one and then another of their village friends.

I never saw Mother more delighted. She watched the Indians' every move, chuckling to herself. All too soon this precious interlude was over; Mother was back in her little apartment, and Rachel was on a plane to Berlin with her monolingual Auca companions. I learned later that the Lord used those two men mightily as, by interpretation, they testified what God had done and what He was doing in their jungles.

15.

Valley in the Sun

For seventeen years, Ruth and I had adjusted our way of life to Ruth Ellyn's needs, and in Argentina this meant that Ruth could hardly ever leave the city. We simply forgot about vacations, but after our Pale Little Flower's home-going we decided as a family to take a camping trip to some isolated spot. We would use a tent and cook our own meals for two whole weeks! The only question was, where to go?

A fellow missionary had told us of a wide valley on the other side of the mountain range whose jagged silhouette can be seen from Cordoba. He said that the road was very narrow and rocky, often with a precipice on one side and a cliff on the other. He assured us, however, that the place was well worth the effort of getting there—an open country, with a few little hamlets and some scattered houses. It all sounded attractive, so we packed clothes, blankets, fishing tackle, and cooking equipment, and started out.

The road was worse than we had imagined, with hundreds of hairpin curves. It offered almost no room anywhere to pass an oncoming car, and fortunately we met almost none. Up, up, and up we climbed, and came out at last on an undulating mesa top. The road down the other side was equally bad, dusty, dangerous, and covered with loose stones, but in the late afternoon we reached a well-paved country road. This led us to a large, deep lake that was formed by a power dam. The lake was flanked on one side by a fishing club and a few houses. The rest of the shoreline was entirely empty. Rocky terrain, scrub trees, and thorn bushes bordered the whole lake.

Here was the solitude we wanted! It was enhanced by the pure mountain air, and exploring would give me the relaxation I needed, along with exercise.

Day after sunny day I wandered off across the rock-strewn, grassy area surrounding the lake. On one such ramble I found myself looking down into a hidden valley. Below me were several cleared fields separated by ancient thorn hedges which had turned black with age. The fields surrounded an adobe "rancho" whose straw-thatched roof was falling in. There was also one crude outbuilding made of small, twisted tree trunks plastered with mud. A lone weeping willow showed above a clump of smaller trees near the buildings.

Mildly curious, I made my way down to the valley floor. The rancho was a sorry sight, with old bones and broken bottles lying about. Cows had used the dark rooms as a refuge from storms, and the dirt floors were thick with their droppings. Cobwebs heavy with dust festooned the walls. Columns of ants and other insects crawled along the smoke-blackened ceilings.

I sat down to think. The place just might have possibilities for a young people's summer camp, with cleared fields close to a big lake in a nearly uninhabited area. All of the four other power-dam lakes that I had seen were already built up with chalets, motels, bars, nightclubs, and marinas. The wild, rugged beauty of this spot excited me.

I got to my feet and began looking for a well; there had to be one somewhere. I discovered two, both of them choked with mud and debris. The grassy glade sloped away gently from the old shack and its fields. The lake itself was a ten-minute walk away.

"Too far!" I thought. The only practicable way to reach this valley would be by boat to the nearest landing place. Afterward, there'd be the ten-minute haul for needed equipment. There was no road in, no electricity, no running stream. Perhaps I should look for a more likely spot, with at least some usable buildings already on it . . .

The Lord kept leading my thoughts back to the hidden valley. I seemed to be entrapped in a mental and spiritual quandary: how to start even a camping site with nothing—*nothing!* I didn't even know who owned this abandoned goat ranch, two kilometers from the nearest road. The wells didn't look sufficient for more than one family, even if they were cleaned out. The buildings were worse than useless. On the other hand, there were very great assets, in the lake and in the view of central Argentina's highest mountains, not to mention the valley's unspoiled isolation.

Committing the whole matter to the Lord, I decided to try to find the owner of this property. That would be a first step.

Of course, at that time I was thinking in terms of perhaps thirty young people sleeping in pup tents and cooking out under a tin-roofed shed. In my letters to the states I wrote about rough cabins of wood and canvas, about country-style outhouses, and a minimum of financial outlay. I didn't dream in my wildest flights of fancy of what the Lord had planned to do here.

I found the owners of the abandoned rancho—a family of the old school. There were four direct heirs: the widowed grandmother, her daughter who was a schoolteacher, and two sons, one a doctor and the other a colonel. In the end they agreed to sell us roughly half of the entire rock-rimmed area, including the open fields and the wells. This amounted to about fifty city blocks of unimproved terrain.

When the natives heard of our purchase, they thought I was crazy. Today many of them think I am a "genius." The difference is what God has brought into being. We began putting in stone foundations, using loose rock from the fields and hillsides. We planted hundreds of shade trees. Little by little, brick cabins and motels took shape. A large central building was erected with lovely white columns on the wide front porch. At the present writing there is a good gravel road into the property, and a private high-tension electric power line to the buildings. One of the wells has been deepened to tap an underground stream so full of water that two powerful centrifugal pumps working together have not been able to empty it.

Much honest sweat, besides a good many tears, has gone into the whole project; but far more important to its progress have been the earnest prayers and faithful giving of our many friends in the states. Like all the growth of the Spanish Evangelistic Crusades, this Bible Conference Center in the geographic heart of Argentina has been a work of faith. God has met each need and guided each forward step in answer to believing prayer. To recount all His answers would require a book by itself, but I must mention a single instance here.

Once I wrote to Ruth Hood, who managed our home office for more than ten years, that we needed seven hundred dollars. By faith she wrote a check, knowing that it would not come back to the bank for about ten days. A few days later a certain businessman telephoned the office to ask if he might help. Ruth Hood suggested that a loan of seven hundred dollars would be quite welcome. He made a gift of that amount.

God's wonderful provision and protection have been evident from the very first at Lake Valley. One day, about five o'clock in the afternoon, I came past the main building with many problems on my mind. Among other things, there was no electricity. The man who had promised to have the line in operation by the fifteenth of December had failed to do so, even though we had paid him promptly as the work progressed. We still had to use small gasoline engines to pump water from the two wells. One motor had broken down, and Haroldo, our handyman, had been working night and day to rig up the small diesel tractor to operate one of the pumps. The water shortage, at that time, was just one of the headaches wearing me down as I tried to provide for the campers' many needs.

Suddenly all my problems lost their importance. Conference guests were standing around in little knots, with anxiety stamped on every face. Something had happened—?

"What's going on?" I asked the nearest group.

"A twelve-year-old boy who went swimming with us is missing," one told me. "He went to the lake with the rest of the swimmers, but he hasn't come back," somebody else volunteered.

An older man with snow-white hair shook his head slowly. "My wife and I were the last ones to leave the swimming area," he said in a tone that was meant to be reassuring. "I checked carefully, and there was no one still in the water when we left."

Somewhat relieved, I walked rapidly down the road to the lake, thinking, "The boy might have tried to return to camp by a different route and gotten lost. In that case somebody could have seen him leave."

I asked campers who were returning to the lake. All they could tell me was that the boy's sneakers and life jacket had been found on a big rock at the edge of the water. This news caught at my throat. I recalled the announcement, made several times each week, that no one was to go into the lake without a life jacket on, or at least an inner tube, because the shoreline drops sharply into deep water and there is no gradual beach. I had labored hard to have two new swimming pools ready; but for lack of funds only the children's pool was usable . . .

Reaching the water's edge, I found a number of young men probing the dark depths with a long pole. Others were diving from a rowboat. More than afraid that the boy's drowned body was down there, I stripped to my swimming trunks and waded in. I dove as deep as I could, searching the shadows for what I hoped I would not see. I tried different areas before deciding that, until expert skin divers with powerful searchlights arrived, our efforts would be hopeless.

Leaving the water, I went to the weeping mother, Doña Marie Dagoberto, and said what few words of encouragement I could manage. Then I returned to camp and sent a camper with a message to the nearest telephone, eight kilometers away—a plea for a frogman to come as soon as possible.

At suppertime everybody's voice was lowered, and little food was eaten. One family which had just arrived left, badly shaken, as soon as they heard the tragic news. Doña Marie kept long vigil at the lake with a woman friend until the other campers met for a spontaneous prayer meeting. Then in the presence of us all she began to pray aloud. I don't recall her exact words, but I remember that she committed her precious boy to the Lord Jesus. She told the Lord that whatever the outcome might be, she would accept His will and love and serve Him just the same.

The loss of our Ruth Ellyn helped me to understand what Doña Marie was going through, but still I was amazed by the strength of her faith. Her voice was charged with emotion, but it was firm. She gave glory to God, Who "doeth all things well"; and when she had finished, the hush was broken by low sobs from her fellow worshipers.

Señor Dagoberto finally arrived by plane, and then, after what seemed like endless waiting, two professional divers. These were powerfully built men, trained for such help as we required. We explained to them that the lad did not know how to swim, but had told others that he was going to dive in headfirst, just like the other children. "Bocha" was large for his age, surcharged with energy and confidence, but he was not accustomed to bathing in a lake. The older person who was acting as lifeguard did not see him dive; and although the spot was surrounded by some fifty bathers, no one noticed that the boy didn't come up again.

The frogmen, in five minutes of diving with their penetrating flashlights, found the body. It was sitting upright, far down in the darkness. The hands were lifted, the eyes closed, the features relaxed as if in prayer.

The child's father stood in silent grief, as the black-clad divers gently laid his son's body on a canvas sheet and covered it, leaving only the face exposed. Doña Marie knelt down, tenderly stroked her boy's cold cheek and talked softly to him, as if he were only asleep. There was no loud wailing, no desperate refusal to accept the fact of death. Tears and a breaking heart, yes! All of us who were watching felt awed. The skin divers shook their heads, almost in unbelief. "We have never seen such faith and composure," one of them told us. "Never, in all our experience retrieving scores of bodies!"

The only wailing heard was that of a humble country woman who lived a kilometer or so from our camp, but she realized quickly that this was out of place, and stopped. That night, after the body had been taken to the hospital's morgue, we debated whether we should have our regular meeting or not. The dead boy's parents were firm: the meeting must continue. Their little lad was a real Christian who loved the Lord. We would see him again, in the glorious Presence of the King. Now we must sing, pray, and study the Word of God even more earnestly than before.

We did, and we all felt better.

Now there is a plot in a quiet country cemetery where "Bocha's" remains await the resurrection morning. To the west stretch broad plains; to the east, rising tier upon tier, loom the guardian mountains. And over the whole countryside word has run like wildfire among those who have lived in superstitious dread of death: that here a father, a mother, and a sister found their faith in the Savior sufficient when tragedy struck.

What could, in other circumstances, have meant a lawsuit and a sudden end of Lake Valley's ministry had now become a spiritual beacon. It is faith like that of "Bocha's" family which testifies to the reality of Christ's power, not only to save the soul but to give victory in the hour of great loss.

None of our problems at camp was as disturbing as a division which marked the first two weeks of our opening summer at camp, however. While some campers were seeking more from the Lord and finding great joy in praising Him from a love-filled heart, others were forming a clique determined to "rescue" me from this "new element" that was upsetting traditional patterns. The split grew daily, and I was in the middle, trying to keep peace in the "family."

One night at a campfire meeting under the trees, a message was given on the text: "Lift up the hands which hang down, and the feeble knees" (Heb. 12:12). The sermon was inspiring and doctrinally sound, but the speaker suggested at the end that we all raise our hands in prayer to the Lord. Of course this smacked of Pentecostalism in the minds of some who were present, an emotionalism that was forbidden in most evangelical circles. To complicate things, one girl of humble background and highly emotional nature began to pray aloud and to cry in a quavering voice. Immediately several girls got up and disappeared into the night. I knew that they were headed for the dining hall to report to the clique which opposed the work the Holy Spirit was doing in many hearts.

I was sure that God was blessing around the fire that night, and I felt that I had to go and make an effort to straighten things out with the "other group." When I got there I found them all upset.

Some were crying, many were jabbering all at once, and I was really nervous. This was the first time I had faced such an issue, but the Lord kept me outwardly calm.

"Let's sit down and thrash this thing out," I suggested.

About half-a-dozen of us sat down around a table. One of the girls who had been at the campfire said that it was like a spiritist seance she had once attended. Since I had never attended one myself I could not refute her accusation. I readily agreed that the simple-minded señorita had been out of order, but I assured everyone that I would talk to her so that she would not repeat her "performance." When others at the table objected to raising hands while praying, I cited King Solomon (I Kings 8:22). Apparently many people in Argentina and elsewhere have not taken time to study the Bible references to this practice, for there are a number of places in the Old Testament, not to mention I Timothy 2:8, where lifting hands to God in prayer is mentioned with approval. I did grant, however, that the campfire speaker might have been more tactful. I felt that what he had asked us to do had scriptural precedent, but that it should not be insisted upon, under the circumstances.

At this point in our discussion, one of the ladies recalled, "Don Felipe, you said at the campfire that you had sinned in not opening your heart long ago to the whole truth of the Holy Spirit." She continued earnestly, "God has wonderfully blessed your ministry. You don't need more than you've got."

She couldn't have been more mistaken. I was to discover over the next few years that God had much more for me than I had yet grasped.

After a few more tearful expressions against "too much emotionalism," the discussion ended on a note of mutual confidence.

Then, one morning, a leading member of our camp organization came to me in a state of great concern. "Don Felipe," he began, "last night a girl in the basement dormitory had a nervous breakdown. They were having a prayer meeting just outside the basement door, and this girl began to weep and carry on something awful!"

I learned that he had been standing about thirty yards away with others who were looking for evidence of "disorderliness." So I went searching for the girl in question. I found her sitting quietly on a bench, waiting for the others to come to the regular morning meeting. She was reading her Bible. Without preamble I said, "I understand that last night you had a nervous breakdown."

The girl looked at me, startled. "Why, no," she responded. "Last night, when we were praying, the Lord was really present; and for the first time in my life I realized the truth about myself. Up until then all I had ever done with my life had been to waste it in selfish, worldly pleasures. When this came home to me I broke down and wept—that's all!"

"And how do you feel this morning?" I asked her.

Her smile was like sunshine bursting through the clouds.

"Oh, I'm so happy, now that I've surrendered completely to the Lord!" she exclaimed.

This, of course, is what revival is all about, and I knew it. But the opposition, already strong, continued to grow. We began to pray more earnestly that the Lord would take full control of our whole camp; and it was not long before He did. Within a few days the grandmother of one of the opposition families took sick. All of them piled into their car and returned to the city. One other ringleader remained, and I felt with deep regret that I must ask him to leave. When he had gone, with his family, a marvelous spirit of harmony and love filled the camp, and since then there has been no more disunity.

16.

The Spiritual Earthquake
Begins

Ready answers have always been formulated to explain the absence of spiritual power in the churches and the lack of respect for Christianity in the secular world. Until now I had not really faced the problem; but my son David, a serious boy just finishing his high school studies, was beginning to question the pat formulas. He saw too many of his age group who were not following the "sound doctrine" with which they had been reared, at least, not in spirit. Carnal, unchristian attitudes lay just under their thin veneer of Biblical correctness. Moreover, the apathy of older churchmen toward their own children's spiritual needs—not to mention the community's—deeply disturbed him.

Too busy with my own organizational work and its problems, I was not aware of David's restlessness until one night when he mentioned at the supper table that he would like to visit a certain Pentecostal church across town. This set me a bit on edge. Of course, in my evangelistic campaigns, I had permitted these "offbeat" sects to cooperate with me. Then, however, they were coming to hear *me* preach. David's wanting to hear *them* preach was something of a shock.

Often a physical earthquake begins with slight tremors that it is possible to ignore. This happens in the spiritual realm, too. So, trying to sound casual, I responded, "Look, son, you are the logical one to open our prayer service here this evening. It just isn't right," I continued, studying David's face, "to go chasing off somewhere when you are needed next door. You know, there are too many 'church tramps' running here and there and shirking responsibility."

"*Sí*, papa," my boy replied, looking at his plate. He was always obedient and respectful. That night he led the singing next door, but he did not give up his desire to visit a Pentecostal meeting. He brought the matter up again, and this time, I replied, "I think I'll go with you." I was concerned lest David should be carried away with the excessively emotional atmosphere he might find there. So we went, together.

The song service was lively. The people clapped their hands as they sang. David clapped and sang likewise, which alerted me to the fact that this was not the first time he had been in such a meeting. Testimonies followed the singing, one given by a day laborer, another by a housewife, still others by young people. Their words were impressive, spoken with enthusiasm and liberally showered with Amens and Hallelujahs.

I didn't particularly mind the hearty Amens, but when the missionary called them all forward to the altar, bedlam broke out in the little hall. One man was especially blessed with a powerful set of lungs and vocal chords of tempered steel. You could hear him above the screeching and moaning of the others. My poor head was in a whirl!

"Dave, old boy," I said, as we reached the sidewalk afterward, "there is just one way to describe what we saw and heard tonight: confusion and disorder!"

When he mentioned the glowing testimonies, I made the standard retort, which probably had some value: "Son, you don't know these people personally. Likely the same ones 'get right with God' at the same altar, night after night. What they say may be wonderful; but unless you know how they live you mustn't jump to conclusions."

Shortly thereafter the missionary left for good, and a fine Pentecostal national pastor took over. He quickly instructed the humble people of the congregation to avoid carnal emotional excesses without dampening true Spirit-imparted ardor. The work began at once to flourish.

After finishing high school, David, with my blessing, left for Buenos Aires to attend the Alliance Bible Institute, from which Martha, our eldest daughter, had graduated. Martha was still in that city, busy and happy with her Argentine husband Sam. She played her accordion and taught Bible to children and young people's groups, while Sam preached. Sam also managed a bookstore and a tract ministry by mail. They amazed Ruth and me by the strength of their faith, as they began traveling on a shoestring, going first to Chile, then to other South American countries, and finally to the United States and the Middle East. Little Stevie, our grandson, was tucked under an arm and taken along. His solemn, wide, blue-gray eyes took in everything as the three of them traveled from place to place.

In the states, Sam preached in Spanish, while Martha interpreted. Between times, he rapidly picked up English. In the Middle East he used his mother's tongue, Greek, and that of his father, Armenian. We followed their travels rather closely, and I noted that, while in the states, Sam and Martha held a good number of meetings in Pentecostal churches. More tremors, warning me of a spiritual upheaval, were soon to be felt!

Meanwhile David was doing very well at school. More than that, he was buying extra books, gradually building up a library of excellent research volumes. When he came home on vacation, we noticed that our tall redhead was constantly seeking out his old pals and talking to them about spiritual things. He spent hours in prayer. At any hour of the day or at night we might hear a low murmur coming from his little room. Now and then such preoccupation with the things of God gave me a little twinge of conscience, as I rushed about with a sheaf of important papers in my hand, or hurried to the telephone, arranging a big campaign. Of course, it was most essential to keep our organization running smoothly—or was it?

One night David joined us for prayer in our bedroom. He stood at the foot of the bed, while Ruth and I knelt. I prayed in Spanish, as I had done from the time of our arrival in Argentina. Ruth, though she had real facility in Spanish, preferred to pray in English. Her prayer followed mine, but while she prayed I was aware of David's low murmuring.

"Strange," I thought, for we were accustomed to listen to one another. I stole a quick glance. David had his face lifted toward heaven and his hands were partly raised. I was struck by the expression on my son's face, one of complete absorption. And then it dawned on me that his words were neither Spanish nor English. *David was praying in an unknown tongue!*

After my first shock had passed, I listened intently. I had always imagined that when a person spoke in an unknown tongue he was seized by a convulsive ecstasy; but David's praying was neither loud nor frenzied, nor could I sense any "vain repetition." Could it be possible, I wondered, that Satan had given our boy a spurious joy, a counterfeit peace which would later sweep him on to the shipwreck of his faith in a maelstrom of emotionalism? I decided to have a talk with him when our prayer time was over.

If David sensed that I was on edge, he gave no sign of it. He quietly affirmed that praying in a "tongue" was entirely scriptural, and that there were thousands of non-Pentecostals who prayed in tongues daily. He pointed out the other gifts that the Holy Spirit desires to give the church; and he spoke of the many instances of divine healing in Buenos Aires as if they were the most natural thing in the world.

"Dad," he said earnestly, "we've never really studied this field of Christian experience. We have simply accepted without question the teaching that these gifts were not for the church today."

I had to grant that point, and I agreed to read some books that David had bought. It was the beginning of a determined investigation. Here was controversial, possibly dangerous ground; but since my son appeared to be deeply involved in this, it behooved me to be fully informed.

David, when a small child, had solemnly stepped out to accept Christ in one of my meetings in North Carolina years before. I had been used of God to lead him into spiritual truth; now it was David's turn to help me!

At about this same time authentic reports began coming to my attention that a new charismatic "movement" had appeared and was gaining incredible strength, throughout Argentina and all of South America. David assured me that the phenomenon was much in evidence in the United States, in fact, all over the world; so also was the controversy that their growth stirred up.

One group of Christians declared that God was sending a marvelous renewal of the Holy Spirit such as the apostles experienced at Pentecost. They reported that a number of churches, spiritually sterile and powerless, had suddenly found new vitality and were now filled with people—especially young people—whose sole and dynamic interest was to live for God and praise His Name. This was the promised "latter rain," the last great revival before the return of Christ. These believers, in the current language of youth, were "turned on." They glowed with a consuming enthusiasm. Some of them had been wholly indifferent to the things of God, others rebellious "dropouts" from the established pattern, religious or social. Now they were giving themselves to much prayer and to meetings that went on for hours, with nobody wanting to go home.

On the other side were those who vehemently accused the new movement of dividing churches and disrupting the work of God, of being disorderly, turning worship services into crazy, noisy confusion. Some went so far as to declare this a sign of the end of the age, when Satan would "transform himself into an angel of light," and thus "deceive many."

I determined not to base any decisions on hearsay, or on others' opinions. As a first step I would go to my Bible, and rethink my long-cherished doctrines in the light of God's Word. I would ask Him alone to direct my study, but I would consider what great spiritual leaders of the past had thought and experienced in the field of charismatic gifts. Afterward, I would visit some of the centers of this new "revival" and observe their fruits.

No amount of willpower can instantly erase a lifelong bias. In this fresh study I clung to the "sound doctrine" that I'd never before questioned: that, since Pentecost, there is no "baptism with the Holy Ghost" to be received following conversion. I clung to it until overwhelming evidence from Holy Scripture wrenched it away.

There was the case of the Samaritan believers, stated so clearly in the eighth chapter of Acts. Philip "preached Christ unto them," wrought miracles of healing, and many people were converted and baptized with water. "And there was great joy in the city." Afterward Peter and John were sent there from Jerusalem, and prayed for these *believers* "that they might receive the Holy Ghost (For as yet He was fallen upon none of them: only they were baptized in the name of the Lord Jesus). Then laid they their hands on them, and they received the Holy Ghost."

I could not escape the force of this sequence of events. What happened after Peter and John had prayed and laid their hands on the converted, Christian Samaritans was quite separate from their experience of salvation or rebirth.

Another clear case was Saul's conversion on the Damascus Road. The first words that Ananias spoke to blinded Saul of Tarsus, right after Saul's encounter with the risen Christ, convinced me beyond all theological quibbling that being "filled with the Spirit" is never to be confused with Christian regeneration or rebirth. Acts 9:17 reads: "And Ananias went his way and entered into the house; and putting his hands on him said, '*Brother* Saul, the Lord, even Jesus, that appeared unto thee in the way as thou camest, hath sent me, that thou mightest receive thy sight, and be filled with the Holy Ghost.' "

"*Brother* Saul!" To me it seemed obvious that, if being "filled with the Spirit" and being saved are synonymous, Ananias would not have called Saul "brother" until *after* he had laid hands on the blinded man and the latter had been filled with the Spirit. Saul undoubtedly had yielded his heart and mind to Christ three days before Ananias entered the house. He was already regenerated, and had even been granted a vision by the Lord. He was already "a chosen vessel" of Christ's (v. 15). But in order to carry out the great work God had planned for him, Saul needed to be "filled with the Spirit."

In Matthew 28:18, our risen Lord told His disciples: "All power is given unto Me in heaven and in earth. Go ye *therefore*," He continued, "and teach all nations." Plainly the disciples were to go in the power of the risen Christ—*a power that they did not yet possess!* For in Luke 24:49, He said: "And, behold, I send the promise of My Father upon you; but tarry ye in the city of Jerusalem, until ye be endued with power from on high."

Why the need for this power? Acts 1:8 is the answer: "Ye shall receive power after that the Holy Ghost is come upon you: and ye shall be witnesses unto Me both in Jerusalem, and in all Judea, and in Samaria, *and unto the uttermost part of the earth*." Now, I reasoned, it would be impossible for these disciples, in their lifetime, to "teach all nations," or to witness "unto the uttermost part of the earth." Therefore the need for Pentecostal power would continue until our Lord's return. (See Matt. 24:14.) And the promise of its supply is just as clear. In Acts 2:38–39, Peter tells his heart-smitten hearers: "Repent and be baptized, every one of you in the Name of Jesus Christ for the remission of sins, and ye shall receive the gift of the Holy Ghost. For the promise is unto you and to your children, *and to all that are afar off, even as many as the Lord our God shall call.*"

God's "promise" of Pentecostal power (which effected the conversion of three thousand people that same day) was abundantly fulfilled in apostolic times and beyond. The gospel of Christ's great salvation swept over the known world and turned it "upside down" (Acts 17:6). According to holy scripture, it is a promise to be claimed today, by "all that are afar off, even as many as the Lord our God shall call." This clearly includes us, since we are "afar off," and have been called of God.

After six months of exhaustive study, I was at last convinced of this, at least in theory. But I wanted to hear corroborating testimony from great Christian leaders of the past. I found it easily.

Dr. Reuben A. Torrey, one of the great Baptist theologians and onetime president of Moody Bible Institute, in his book, *How to Bring Men to Christ*, devotes the closing chapter to this special anointing for service. He writes, "What is the Baptism of the Holy Spirit? It is a definite and distinct operation of the Holy Spirit and it is possible to know whether its effectiveness has been received or not. . . . A person can be regenerate by the Holy Spirit without being baptized by Him. Such a person is saved, but is not fit for the service of Christ. Every believer has the Holy Spirit (Rom. 8:9) but not every believer has the baptism of the Holy Spirit" (Acts 8:12–16).

From a careful study of the lives and teachings of Dwight L.

Moody, Charles Finney, C. T. Studd, F. B. Meyer, Jonathan Goforth, and other noted men of God, it is clear that these held the same view as Dr. Torrey on the infilling of the Holy Spirit. Except for Finney's power-packed experience, I did not come across any direct reference in their writings to speaking in tongues, but they were unanimous in teaching that the essential empowering for service is a crisis experience. It may be coincident with the new birth, but it is more often subsequent to it. During the eighteenth century, when missionary work was at its best, it was quite usual for Christians to seek this baptism (literally "immersion") in the Holy Spirit, for power to serve with greater blessing and effectiveness.

In his biography of C. T. Studd, Norman Grubb writes: ". . . when he definitely applied himself to seek and discover God's plan for his life, the first answer he received from God was a revelation of his own need, and the second, that this need could be met by receiving the fulness of the Holy Spirit. As soon as he saw this in the Scriptures, he received the Holy Spirit as a child, by means of a simple act of complete surrender and faith. He was then properly equipped to answer the calling and go through the trials which followed."

Torrey, reporting on his great and good friend, D. L. Moody, says: "Once he (Moody) had some teachers at Northfield—fine men, all of them; but they did not believe in a definite baptism with the Holy Ghost for the individual. They believed that every child of God was baptized with the Holy Ghost, and they did not believe in any special baptism with the Holy Ghost for the individual. Mr. Moody came to me and said, 'Torrey, will you come up to my house after the meeting tonight, and I will get those men to come, and I want you to talk this thing out with them.'

"Of course, I readily consented, and Mr. Moody and I talked for a long time, but they did not altogether see eye to eye with us.

And when they went, Mr. Moody signaled me to remain for a few moments. Mr. Moody sat there with his chin on his breast, as he so often sat when he was in deep thought; then he looked up and said: 'Oh, why will they split hairs? Why don't they see that this is just the one thing that they themselves need? They are good teachers, and I am so glad to have them here; but why will they not see that the baptism with the Holy Ghost is just the one touch that they themselves need?'

"On Sunday morning I spoke on 'The Baptism in the Holy Spirit: How To Get It.' It was just exactly twelve o'clock when I finished my morning sermon, and I took out my watch and said: 'Mr. Moody has invited us all to go up on the mountain at three o'clock this afternoon to pray for the power of the Holy Spirit. It is three hours to three o'clock. Some of you cannot wait. Go to your rooms; go to your tent; go out into the woods; go anywhere where you can get alone with God and have this matter out with Him.'

"At three o'clock we all gathered in front of Mr. Moody's mother's house (she was then still living) and then began to pass down the lane, through the gate, up on the mountainside. There were four hundred and fifty-six of us in all; I know the number because Paul Moody counted us as we passed through the gate. After a while, Mr. Moody said: 'I don't think we need to go any further; let us sit down here.' We sat down on stumps and logs and on the ground. Mr. Moody said: 'Have any of you students anything to say?' I think about seventy-five of them arose, one after the other, and said: 'Mr. Moody, I could not wait till three o'clock; I have been alone with God since the morning service, and I believe I have a right to say that I have been baptized with the Holy Spirit.'

"When these testimonies were over, Mr. Moody said: 'Young men, I can't see any reason why we shouldn't kneel down here right now and ask God that the Holy Ghost may fall upon us just as definitely as He fell upon the apostles on the Day of Pentecost. Let us pray.'

"And we did pray," says Torrey, "there on the mountainside. As we had gone up the mountainside, heavy clouds had been gathering, and just as we began to pray those clouds broke and the raindrops began to fall through the overhanging pines. But there was another cloud that had been gathering over Northfield for ten days, a cloud big with the mercy and grace and power of God; and as we began to pray our prayers seemed to pierce that cloud and the Holy Ghost fell upon us. Men and women, that is what we all need—the Baptism in the Holy Ghost." As all this came home to me, I decided that I should not be ashamed to take my stand beside such spiritual giants as Moody, Torrey, and C. T. Studd.

My next step was to read the books written by Pentecostals, that my son David, with quiet earnestness, had urged me to consider. The first one was *They Speak with Other Tongues,* by John L. Sherrill. With his dispassionate study of glossolalia, past and present, Sherrill combined a frank and sensitive account of his own spiritual pilgrimage from a nominal Christianity to a living faith, and later to the experience of the Holy Spirit's infilling. Little by little, his analytical mind had grown certain that the Pentecostal movement was in most instances a true and scriptural awakening—not the shallow, emotional "wildfire" that its critics painted.

I still reserved judgment, but I had to ask myself if I had erred in accepting "for doctrines the commandments of men," regarding the charismatic gifts, tongues included. (Cf. Matt. 15:9.)

After reading David Wilkerson's *The Cross and the Switchblade,* I was convinced that here was a man led by God's Spirit. He lived in a supernatural realm of which I knew very little. He had gone, penniless but constrained and sustained by God's power, into the slums of a wicked city where street murder and the practice of every human vice were commonplace. There, by that same Power, he had led vicious gang members, drug addicts, pimps, and streetwalkers to Christ. He'd seen the miracle of salvation take place in hundreds of these derelicts. Upon most of them the Holy Spirit had fallen, along with the gift of tongues; and their change of life was usually permanent. Dave Wilkerson's project, "Teen Challenge," spread to city after city, staffed by Spirit-filled workers who oftentimes had been derelicts before Christ made them over new.

I could not brush Wilkerson off as a deluded heretic. I felt unworthy to shine his shoes.

Months of searching the scriptures, with particular attention to I Corinthians 12–14, together with the study of theological treatments of the subject, finally settled the question for me. *All* of the gifts of the Holy Spirit, including that of speaking in an unknown tongue, must be meant for the Christian today. The only scriptural warning attached to any of them is regarding a selfish or inconsiderate use of "tongues," and of "prophesying," in chapter 14.

These facts have been clearly set forth by Dr. Clark H. Pinnock and Grant R. Osborne in *Christianity Today*. The article that all should read thoughtfully is entitled: "A Truce Proposal for the Tongues Controversy." Two short statements by these Greek scholars merit quoting here: "Moreover, the New Testament nowhere teaches that the gifts were given solely to authenticate the apostles or that they were to cease after the apostolic age." And this succinct observation: "The only cessation (of the gifts of the Spirit) to which he (Paul) refers is that which occurs *at the coming of Christ.*" (italics mine)

I was amazed to read that no less than John Calvin regarded glossalalia as a legitimate gift of the Spirit. Calvin wrote *against* those who "declaim against (unknown tongues) with furious zeal." He said, "Paul, nevertheless, commands the use of tongues. So far is he from wishing them abolished or thrown away."

With this very much in my mind, I went to Buenos Aires to see what was going on there. My first stop was at Quilmes, a suburb of the city. There I found an old friend, Jorge Pradas, at the head of a gospel church that was reliving first century Christianity. A converted actor, Jorge had fled from severe persecution in Spain. He had renounced all connection with the stage until we started making evangelical films together. I had been rather out of touch with Jorge for a while, though rumors of his activities had reached me. Expelled from his Plymouth Brethren Church for holding "false doctrines," he and a number of Spirit-filled members started meeting in a lathe shop. In two years this group of fifteen had grown to a church of over two hundred God-empowered Christians. Their nightly street meetings never saw fewer than half-a-dozen professions of faith. New converts and seekers were bundled into a homemade bus and brought to the church for another lively meeting filled with the joy of the Lord.

The amazing growth of Jorge's church—with which I became well acquainted—was fairly typical of the revivals that I found in other parts of Buenos Aires. Most groups were a bit quieter in worship than the Quilmes church, but in each there was a wonderful spirit of joy and love. Since everyone tithed his income, there was always money for missions, money for the new church building, money for whatever needed to be done for the glory of God.

In one church I visited, the men began studying the Book of Acts together. From time to time they stopped and asked themselves, "Are *we* doing this?" More often than not the answer was, "No."

"Then, let's do it!" they agreed. Since the early Christians prayed (Acts 4:29–30), "Lord . . . grant unto thy servants that with all boldness they may speak thy word, by stretching forth thine hand to heal; and that signs and wonders may be done by the name of thy holy child Jesus," these earnest men began praying the same prayer. They read how the apostles and others laid hands on the sick, and the sick recovered; so they, too, began laying hands on the sick, and the Lord began healing one after another. They preached, and demonstrated, that the Word of God is as living and powerful as when it was written. Their church came alive and is still growing.

I found that everywhere in Buenos Aires believers were bringing Christ to the man-in-the-street. I was told that six hundred of them met in a park, singing the praises of the Lord and preaching the Word. Just as the Apostle Paul taught "publicly and from house to house" (Acts 20:20), so I found awakened Christians meeting in many small, informal groups in private houses, inviting their uncommitted neighbors to come in for a bit of fellowship. Three or thirty might accept. There was no appearance of a formal meeting. Everyone sat around a table drinking tea and munching cookies. The Christians prayed, and after a few such get-togethers they began to sing simple choruses and to engage in more serious Bible study.

While there was no formality in these small outreach meetings, the leaders whom I interviewed told me that there was a plan. Their pastor carefully prepared each of his most spiritual men to lead and direct one or more groups, passing on what he had learned. In turn, some members of each group began directing their own, each finding disciples who could teach others. So, given a vital task, each believer became more vital, "holding forth the Word of Life."

Some neighbors, I learned, were well-converted long before they ever sat in a regular church service. As fast as each one came into the full light of salvation, he was taken to the church and baptized, as promptly as was the Philippian jailer. The baptistry was kept ready night and day, and the lay believers baptized those whom they personally led to the Lord. There were even cases where a bathtub served as a baptistry! One church in Buenos Aires has over three hundred home study groups meeting each week!

My firsthand contact with this new "charismatic movement" shook me to the depths of my soul, in a way most difficult to describe. It recalled a flight that I had once made over Brazil's *Mato Grosso*. Below us, rising from the limitless green of the forest, was a small plateau, its green top borne up on mile-high, gray-brown cliffs; and down those cliffs I could see thirty or more white, feathery waterfalls cascading from the immense height. All at once its sudden upthrust seemed duplicated in the air that bore up our plane. A terrific updraft seized us. Lightning flashed, illuminating dark, eerie cloud masses which loomed like the walls of an unearthly cavern. We rose almost vertically—then were driven down as if by a giant's fist. I was certain the ship's wings would be torn off. Rain roared against the fuselage. The plane twisted, leaped, and fell like an elevator with its cable snapped. At last it staggered out into fairly quiet air.

I had been swept by force of circumstances into a theological vortex. Here, in Buenos Aires, I tried to fight my way to calmer air, mentally and spiritually; but more turbulence lay ahead.

17.

God Begins a New Work

Fellowship with the awakened believers in Buenos Aires had given me a startling glimpse of my own spiritual need. It made me thirst for more of God, "as the hart panteth after the water brooks" (Psa. 42:1). Now the Holy Spirit began probing deeply, forcing me to think back over the years of my ministry and take careful inventory.

I saw that I had been guilty of comparing myself with other Christians around me; and with that natural pride which grows like an ugly weed in the soul, I had concluded that my life and ministry were above the average, and therefore satisfactory. Now God was holding up a mirror that showed me a life spiritually retarded, incomplete, and far from what He wanted it to be.

To be sure, God had challenged Christians through my ministry. He had blessed my preaching of His Word. He had used it to save souls. Yet while certain aspects of my work for Him showed divine strength and grace, others were woefully lacking. Over the years, our Lord had tried to bring these grave deficiencies to my attention; but my self-satisfaction and my habit of forging on under full sail had blinded me to the storm signals flying from many masts.

What I saw now, like a half-finished building against a flaming sunset, was my life edifice racked with weaknesses and wasted effort. I could pick out all the shaky rafters and sagging joints in that pitiless light.

It was abundantly clear that, along with a sincere desire to preach the gospel and "win souls," I had nursed a carnal wish to be a "successful" evangelist in the eyes of my peers. It was plain that much of my criticism of believers had been an effort to exalt self. My hidden wish had been for others to honor me as a prominent defender of the truth.

Shame crushed my heart! I recalled, too, how often I had turned off into personal bypaths, promoting my own schemes, to the detriment of the work God had entrusted to me.

My life, and my ministry, needed a major work of renovation by that same Holy Spirit Whose power had transformed Dwight L. Moody, Reuben A. Torrey, Jorge Pradas—yes, and my own son David, not to mention the groups of God-empowered Christians I had met in Buenos Aires. Not regeneration: since I gave my heart to Jesus as a child, the Holy Spirit had been living in me, and I had been "a new creature in Christ." What I needed was to be *immersed in Him,* filled as a cup that is dipped deep in the ocean!

Somewhere along this line of thought and study the Lord gave me other illustrations of the difference between the "indwelling" of the Spirit and His "infilling—" to show how He Who already indwells could later "come upon" those who sought the "baptism." On our summer conference property we had two wells. In one of them was an abundance of water. From time to time, massive storm clouds would form over the mountains just beyond our lovely valley, and their wind-borne downpour would come upon us with a mighty roar. It was water, the same element that was in the well; but this deluge was overwhelming. Thus God the Holy Spirit can nourish our life as from a pure well; and He can also come upon us from above, so that we "may . . . be filled . . . with God himself" (Eph. 3:19 Phillips).

This I must seek. My son-in-law, Sam, who had received this baptism, said something which prodded me on: "You cannot go any farther now in preaching this truth until you possess *as a present reality* that which your heart believes in." He was right; yet in the back of my mind was the nagging thought, "If all this is true, what about my relationship with those who reject it categorically? Some of them will certainly excommunicate me, and they are my dear friends in Christ! Financial support will be cut off. Consternation, even confusion, will spread among those who look to me as a teacher of sound doctrine . . ." But God's truth compelled me to go on. I would seek the fullness of the Holy Spirit, trusting Him to round out my partial experience and my limited ministry.

I began by seeking the gift of speaking in tongues, as well. While I felt that this gift might not be absolutely essential to the "baptism in the Spirit," I knew that in New Testament times it was generally the case that those who received His "anointing" also spoke in tongues. I believed that the gift would prove to be an added blessing to my ministry. I began to pray to this end.

For a while at camp, several of us went out every day to a quiet spot among the trees, to pray. One day my only companion was Jorge Pradas. As we strolled down the shady path among the thorn trees, I recalled Jorge's telling me how he had received the baptism, not long before, while standing on the street in town. He had claimed by faith the saying of Christ: ". . . how much more shall your Heavenly Father give the Holy Spirit to them that ask Him?" (Luke 11:13). Jorge had asked, and the Lord had answered with waves of blessing that bathed his soul with holy joy. He did not speak in tongues at that time, but several weeks later, as he prayed, there came from his lips in the most natural way a flood of adoration in a new language.

When we reached a bit of pasture off the beaten path I said, "Jorge, I believe God wants me to receive by faith this fullness. I believe He wants to bless me with the gift of tongues as well."

He looked at me with complete understanding as I went on: "In the Bible, time and again, it says that the apostles laid hands on them and they received the Holy Spirit, in this special sense. So I want you to place your hands on my head and pray."

I thought for a moment, sensing the presence of my Lord, then continued, "I'm going to forget all my successes and failures, all my long years of preaching and all my theological studies. I'm going to place myself before the Lord like a little child—make a fool of myself if necessary, but I'm going to take a step of faith, just like those priests of Israel who put their feet in the Jordan River, long years ago, trusting God to open a way for them."

I knelt while Jorge placed his hands on my head and began to pray softly in Spanish, with a few phrases in tongues. Then I began to pray. At first it was little more than stammering, but very soon it came clearer. The nearness of the Lord was thrilling. The sense of peace and joy was strong. For a minute or two I prayed effortlessly, clearly, in what sounded like a definite language. Then I changed into Spanish, thanking my Heavenly Father for adding this new gift to the others He had already given. Jorge rejoiced with me, and we continued in prayer for a good while.

From that time on, I have prayed almost daily in Spanish and tongues. To invent what I was speaking would have been a tiring if not impossible task. What I did experience was a restful, spiritually edifying communication, just as the Apostle Paul said it should be.

I already know that speaking in tongues was not the important issue. It was not so much the "gift" as the Giver that mattered. It was my Lord Jesus Who had baptized me with the Holy Ghost, as John the Baptist had prophesied. In an act of faith I had definitely rejected man's teaching, severed strong ties of tradition, and accepted God's truth. This was to have powerful repercussions in my ministry.

Cutting the rope which fastens a boat to the wharf may seem a small act. Its true importance appears when a surging current seizes and sweeps the craft away. I had cut loose from a static, human doctrine to move with the flow of God's Spirit toward all that He purposed for my life. From that moment my horizons changed.

One evidence of God's new work within me was the sense of peace. Previously, when I met with strong opposition, I was nervous and afraid. (An artist's temperament, quick to react!) Now I found that I could meet sticky situations—and people—without a thumping heart, sweaty palms, and hesitant speech. My amazement reminded me, "This is the Lord's doing; it is marvellous in our eyes" (Psa. 118:23).

Ruth, too, had been seeking the Lord's fullness, and in a time of prayer in our home with old friends had asked for the gift of tongues. It did not come until a godly brother suggested that she pray in English first instead of in Spanish. This seemed to release her from a limitation, and at once she was praying in tongues. However, the experience did not return as a continued blessing until later on. Nothing has done more to close the "generation gap" in our family than this thrilling renewal experience. The Holy Spirit has knit us together in a way we never knew before. Love fills our hearts for one another, humility marks our home relationships, and divine wisdom guides our steps as we walk together in His ways. Even though our son-in-law Sam and daughter Martha are far away in the Middle-east with their two darling children, our oneness in the Spirit is very real and precious. Evelyn, now thirteen, is happily united with us in all our service for

Christ, delighted with the buoyant spirit of joy in the meetings, and completely unsullied by the filth and smut of her teenage environment. She has found that "this is where it is at."

Soon after my baptism in the Spirit, we felt led to start a prayer and praise service for all those who wanted to seek the Lord's gifts in the new light of understanding that He had poured into our hearts. We opened the studio of our building in Cordoba, and soon between twenty and thirty people were coming each Monday night. We chose Monday so as not to interfere with the usual church meetings. Our purpose was not to draw believers away from their churches, but rather to see them catch fire with a spiritual revival that they could take back with them, to church and to daily business. Its reality would show in Christ-filled lives.

Very shortly, rumor reached the nearby church of which I was a member in fellowship, that I was forming a new church, a competitive one. So, at the close of one Sunday morning worship service I went forward, with perfect quietness of heart, and spoke to the congregation.

"The Monday-night prayer meeting," I said, "is not the beginning of a rival group. We are not starting a new church. Whenever I feel God's call to start another local work, it will be in some neighborhood where there is no Christian witness at all." (There are many neglected areas in Cordoba.)

One leader asked me if this Monday-night group were similar to one which was meeting a thousand strong in Buenos Aires. "I think so," I replied.

Later on, long letters came from the capital to the church board, urging that I be thrown out. The accusations were that I was teaching "false doctrine" and consorting with Pentecostals. I had two meetings with the board. In one of them a distinguished leader first made it clear that he was not related to the new movement, and then offered this opinion, as I recall it.

"We Plymouth Brethren," he said, "have taught for years that each local group is autonomous and answerable to God alone. How, then, are we going to accede to the demands of leaders in Buenos Aires and expel Don Felipe, the founder of this church?"

After some more discussion the rest agreed; and although no direct action was taken against me, I was no longer invited to minister the Word there. Their restrained attitude impressed me, but what meant far more was the fact that through the whole affair I felt absolutely no fear or nervousness.

Along with my spiritual earthquake and changed horizons had come God's gift of inward quietness, a peace which continued in the face of strongly written letters and interviews threatening my future as a missionary. Two young ladies who had come to camp from Brazil reported back to stateside missionaries in that country that we were Pentecostal. Apparently others from Argentina had made the same accusation in letters to the states. The alarm spread. One day a short, terse letter came from a longtime friend who was a board member of our mission, saying that he had heard I was "mixed up in this tongues' business," and that I had turned "Pentecostal." I replied at some length, explaining that I wasn't mixed up at all; on the contrary, the Lord was straightening me out, and that what I believed was in the Bible.

I did my best to explain to all that my basic doctrinal position had not changed. Our printed doctrinal statement, similar to many used by Christian colleges and missionary agencies, was still the same. I repeated, over and over again, that tongues was not the important issue. However, it was very important, apparently, to some of my former friends who began cutting off our missionary support. This really hurt; but I knew that I was being true to God's Word and to the Body of Christ.

All sorts of books against the "tongues' movement" began coming to my desk. I read each one carefully, checking its conclusions against the scriptures. Yet it became clearer with each reading that the writers had injected into many passages a meaning which was not there. What they saw as a scriptural disparagement of speaking in tongues was really only a warning against *abuse* of God's gift, and not against its use.

If only I could get across to my friends the thrilling experience that was now mine each day! How could I convince them that this was not mental aberration or shallow emotionalism, but wholesome, satisfying communication with God in an unknown tongue *that He gave me;* and that this was a heart-experience of the Presence of Christ such as I had never known before?

As one after another of them, by letter or face-to-face, expounded his views on "tongues" and the baptism with the Spirit, I felt that they were like blind men talking about color and light.

Once while I was in the states, a certain pastor brought up the idea that a charismatic emphasis tends to downgrade the Person of Christ, referring to Him as "Jesus" instead of as "Lord." I was happy to tell him that in Argentina an outstanding feature of our current revival is the exaltation of Christ as Lord of all, and that Argentine poets and musicians were writing many beautiful choruses (some of which are literally scripture verses set to music) whose central theme is the supreme Lordship of Christ.

In New England, my son David and I enjoyed wonderful fellowship with the pastor of an independent, fundamental, Bible church. During a very earnest conversation, this brother expressed a fear that in many instances Satan transforms himself "into an angel of light," giving people experiences that counterfeit God-given experiences. In such cases the feeling of joy gradually disappears, to be replaced by confusion. The result is a shipwrecked life. The pastor had case histories that confirmed his opinion. He believed in the reality of demon possession today, and had himself cast out evil spirits in the Name of the Lord. In one such instance a young lady had begun to speak in tongues.

"When she told me that she was a tongues' speaker," the pastor explained, "I challenged her to a test that is laid down in the

Word of God." He quoted I Corinthians 12:3: "Wherefore I give you to understand that no man, speaking by the Spirit of God, calleth Jesus accursed: and that no man can say, Jesus is the Lord, but by the Holy Ghost." Then he asked her if she would be willing to pray in an unknown tongue, so that he might ask whatever spirit was moving her to answer him, saying, "Jesus is the Lord."

The young lady agreed, and as she spoke in tongues, he put the question. As he expected, her voice faltered. She stammered and became all confused. Finally from her lips came, "No, no, no!" and she stopped. As a result she gave up tongues.

The pastor asked me if I would be willing to submit to the same test. "If your speaking is by demonic power," he said, "you will not be able to continue, any more than that young lady."

Sincere and direct, his proposal shocked me. "Well," I replied, "for me, praying in tongues is a very personal and private matter. It is not for display."

He did not insist. However, next morning while I was in his office, about to leave for another town, I felt led to submit to the test. I was now certain that we ought to make the test, not for my assurance, but for his. I explained that I would pray first in English, then in Spanish (which was more natural for me), and then in tongues. This I did, the Lord taking away all feeling of embarrassment as I reached out to Him in prayer; and while I was praying in tongues the pastor enjoined the spirit who prayed to declare that "Jesus is Lord."

There was no hesitation—only a deep joy as I exclaimed in English, "Jesus is Lord, Jesus is Lord!" Then I continued praying in tongues. We made a second test with the same result.

While I don't doubt that some have been led astray by Satan, and have been deluded by a spurious emotional experience, I know that what God has given me is beyond doubt or question. And I know hundreds of Argentines who use tongues in their daily devotions. They have not gone astray, nor have their lives been harmed in any way. On the contrary, they are living "all out" for God, their abiding joy expressed in prayer and praise and in soul-winning efforts.

The little group which began in our studio has now grown to several hundred rejoicing believers. We meet in a large auditorium downtown. Those who attend for the first time feel the surge of divine love in our midst. Cultured ladies, greeting the poorest of the poor, kiss them on both cheeks, as is the custom among close relatives. Men and boys of all classes and walks of life throw their arms around each other as warm friends do in Argentina. They bless one another with words of encouragement. We look at one another across the room, and a smile of understanding, of spiritual communion, passes between us.

Lonely, confused teenagers are caught up in this wonderful wave of holy love. They find themselves surrounded by warm-hearted adults who meet their great need for sympathetic understanding. Then the tawdry experiments, the momentary stimulants and gratifications of their mixed-up existence, all drop away. Real life, new, deep and satisfying, begins.

Never—hear me!—*never* have I seen such an outflowing of God's love, or such unity and harmony. It is pure and holy, with no taint of the carnal. Week after week, newcomers are overwhelmed with the spirit of Christ, so evident in the singing and praying. Bible messages throb with compassion. They impart life. They expose sin and unbelief. They exalt Christ. Meetings continue for two hours or more, but no one wants to go home when they close. First Corinthians 13 in practice is a present reality. Throughout Argentina revival has begun. It erases the prejudices that separate Christians of different communions. It levels the barriers between rich and poor.

All who receive the baptism with the Spirit become from that moment brothers in Christ in the fullest sense of the term. They believe in miracles because the anointing they have received is a miracle. When godless people receive the fullness of the Spirit, at salvation or soon afterward, the change in their lives is spectacular.

In my own case, the baptism with the Spirit powerfully intensified what God had already given. It was the overflooding of a well that already contained living water. I had new victory over circumstances and a new influence with people. Love was casting out fear.

A few months after I had experienced this baptism at camp, our team was conducting a campaign away out on those vast plains called the pampa. One day as I went out alone across the barren terrain to pray, the young pastor with whose church we were meeting asked to go with me, and on the way he spoke of a matter that was deeply troubling him. He had expected, when he took this church, to see many souls saved and to see much spiritual growth in the believers there. But this did not happen, and he blamed himself. He lacked what was needed to win souls and see progress. He was profoundly discouraged, and I realized that at this rate he would soon be out of the ministry, utterly defeated.

We sat down in a rocky washout, and there I told him of the joy, the peace, power, and love that was now flooding my life since I had opened my heart to receive the Holy Spirit in His fullness. When I had finished, he said, "This is exactly what I need, dear brother!"

I replied, "This is all very new to me, but if God used Balaam's ass to help a prophet, I am sure he can use me to help you. Let us pray, and I'll lay my hands on you as they did in the apostles' day."

I placed my hands on his head and prayed for him. When I fell silent, he began to pray in Spanish; then there poured from his lips a torrent of words that neither of us could understand. "Joy in the Holy Ghost" was suddenly overflowing our hearts, and the glory of God seemed to fill that rocky gulch.

When the young pastor finally ceased praying in tongues, he threw his arms around me in a bear hug that I thought would crack my ribs. Next day he told me that the gift was still there; and what precious fellowship we enjoyed working together for the rest of the campaign!

With the campaign ended, the tent packed up, and everything ready for the long trip back to Cordoba, the pastor told me of a girl about twelve years old who lived just around the corner. She was mentally disturbed.

"The family is unconverted," he told me, "but I feel that we should go there and pray for her."

We went, and were ushered into a humble bedroom, where the child was curled up on the bed. She recoiled from us, like a kitten surrounded by barking dogs. A terrible fear showed in her black eyes as she cringed against the headboard. We did not approach her; but, standing at the foot of the bed, we prayed, in the name of Jesus, that God would deliver her from all fear and Satanic power—a simple, earnest petition.

Early next day, our team and equipment rolled out of town, homeward bound. And within a week there came a glowing letter from the pastor telling how the Lord had changed his whole ministry. At the close of the letter he mentioned the child we had prayed for. "Next morning," he wrote, "the parents took her to the doctor. He found her to be one hundred percent well, with no trace of the mental disturbances which had been tormenting her."

Thrilling news! Later on I learned that the whole family began coming to church, and, one after another, accepted Christ as their Savior. This was clear confirmation of my belief regarding divine healing and deliverance. It is evidence to the unsaved that the heart of the living Christ is as full of compassion today as when He walked in Galilee; and it often leads to their salvation.

Not everyone for whom I have prayed has been healed. I once prayed for a small boy full of cancer, and there was a definite turn for the better; but later on he died. Was it because the local pastor, instead of standing with me and with the family, denounced them for having asked me to come and pray for their child? I don't know.

Again, I prayed for a man whose legs had been paralyzed when a "hot" electric cable fell across his back. He was so sure he would be healed that he took off his bathrobe and put on a pair of trousers. But strength did not come to his legs. Why? I am not sure. I know that there is power in corporate, united faith. "Where two or three are gathered together in My Name, there am I," said Jesus, "in the midst of them" (Matt. 18:20). If the entire congregation of this man's church had raised believing prayer for his healing, it might have been granted. The question still haunts me.

Christ once said, regarding the demon-possession of a boy who had been brought to his disciples for healing, "This kind goeth not out but by prayer and fasting." How many of us are fasting today? How many are really exercising living faith? I confess my great need in this respect.

Have you noticed in reading the New Testament that the apostles not only prayed for others, but, on occasion, spoke with Christ's authority directly to the person concerned? In Acts 3:6, Peter commanded the crippled man, "In the Name of Jesus Christ of Nazareth, rise up and walk!" And in Acts 9:40, he spoke to the body of a dead believer, "Tabitha, arise!"

Of this I am sure: God's Word is true. "And this is the confidence that we have in Him, that, if we ask anything *according to His will,* He heareth us: and if we know that He hear us, whatsoever we ask, we have the petitions that we desired of Him" (I John 5:14–15).

There are times when "we know not what we should pray for as we ought" (Rom. 8:26), and we have to cast our burden on the Holy Spirit, Who "Himself maketh intercession for us . . . according to the will of God" (Rom. 8:26–27).

There are times when the will of God is crystal clear to us. Obedience may be joyfully confident, or it may cost us untold human anguish. In either case, His Presence, "closer than breathing, nearer than hands and feet," is what counts, as it did a few years ago when Ruth went to the hospital with severe hepatitis.

The doctors did not tell me that they despaired of her life; they just said, "We will have to wait and see." The pain in their eyes, however, told me more than their words.

I was scheduled to leave in a few days for Chile, where veteran missionaries were counting on the help of our team. They were going from house to house, inviting people to the meetings which were soon to begin in the basketball stadium; and they were emphasizing the chalk drawings that the artist would present along with special music. If I failed to appear, it could well be a fatal blow to their campaign, especially since another mission preceding them had left a bad testimony and seriously hurt the evangelical cause. I knew how these faithful servants of Christ longed to see souls saved, lives transformed, and a solid work raised up for God's glory. If I let them down, all their effort and much money would be lost; and, of far more importance, many precious souls would not be reached for the Lord.

When our children were born—almost always late—at the same time that preaching engagements called me away, I had left Ruth to go "through the valley" alone. It was her wish, and my conviction, that God's work should come first. This relapse of hepatitis was a much more dangerous condition; but with her usual courage and strong faith in the Savior's care, she told me,

"Honey, you go, and the Lord will take care of me." And yet
. . . Once on the plane for Chile, I would be without word of her
for several days. Ruth could be in her grave by then.

I vacillated, crying out in agony to my Heavenly Father, seeking clear guidance. But the more I prayed, the more I felt certain
that if I obeyed the Lord and went on to Chile, He would care
for my beloved companion. In this certainty, though still dreading
our separation for the days just ahead, I boarded the plane.

We had a wonderful campaign, and about a hundred and thirty
were soundly converted. Those people who had once received a
bad impression of evangelicals came to have a profound respect
for our work. At the earliest moment after the closing meeting I
was on a plane flying east to Cordoba across the mighty Andes. I
found Ruth out of danger, well on the way to recovery. When I
spoke to the doctors, they told me, wonderingly, "We never expected to see your wife leave this hospital alive." Prayer had made
the difference.

18.

The New Day Brightens

More than ten years have come and gone since I went through Chile's great earthquake; and about five years have passed, at this writing, since God's mighty Hand shook my own spiritual ground. In each cataclysmic upheaval much was changed: familiar, protecting walls crashed in ruin; cherished vistas, even beloved faces, disappeared.

Many believe that what has happened to me has been a tragic departure from "sound" teaching. They feel that I have "gone overboard," deluded by Satan, carried away by strange "winds of doctrine." They are convinced that I have "gotten mixed up in this tongues' business," and have thereby hurled confusion into the ranks of the faithful. Nothing could be further from the truth. Let me summarize what God has done in my life.

For me, all the great Bible-based foundations of faith remain unshaken and unshakable. Only structures of tradition and man-made dogma have crumbled; and in their place is a truer understanding of His Word. The emphasis has changed from *my* local church to the fellowship of all believers; from *my* denomination to the Body of Christ; from *my* group's doctrines to the whole Bible, and to Jesus Christ, the Living Word. He alone is Lord, and what He says is final. This profound assurance has brought a new sense of the Savior's presence into my daily experience. The holy warmth of His divine love renews my spirit. Oh, how precious are the moments that I spend alone with Him!

Christ's presence has shown me my great shortcomings in a new and truer light. I am like the prodigal son who, before his repentance, said to his father, "Give me"; and after his return, humbled and broken, cried, "Father . . . make me!"

Can a "successful" evangelist be shaken out of his self-satisfaction? Can a missionary who has seen much blessing on his ministry learn new patterns of behavior, experience radical changes in his personality? The answer is a great big YES! All my life, I have had a feverish desire for quick action and quick results. I have been like a puppy running ahead of his master, tugging at the leash. Now, all at once, the futile tugging is over. When the Holy Spirit has complete freedom to guide us we are able to hear His "still, small voice" (I Kings 19:11–18) or to wait on the Lord until His will is clearly known.

Earthquakes that take place near the sea usually cause tidal waves. Over my life has come a tidal wave of love, flowing from the heart of Jesus my Lord. It has brought new tenderness toward others. It has created a fresh sensitivity toward their hopes and fears, joys and sufferings, a desire both to share with and to learn from them regardless of what denominational label they may wear. This, of course, is what the Bible exhorts all believers to seek: to "walk worthy of the vocation wherewith ye are called, with all lowliness and meekness, with longsuffering, forbearing one another in love; *endeavoring to keep the unity of the Spirit in the bond of peace*" (Eph. 4:1–3).

Certain friends opposed to this great charismatic revival have intimated that my taking part in it impugns the "faith of our fathers," and is therefore a betrayal of my martyr brother and my godly parents. On the contrary, what God is now doing, for and through me, is the fruit of Dad's and K-Ma's prayers for me. Both of them believed in divine healing through prayer. Both believed in the absolute necessity of being filled with the Holy Spirit. Fa-

ther was converted and set on fire for God through the preaching
of J. Wilbur Chapman, who believed in a special "baptism" for
service. The night Dad was saved, Chapman's sermon text was,
"Have ye received the Holy Ghost since ye believed?" (Acts
19:2). Both my oldest brother and I object.

I shall never forget the last time Dad attended one of my meetings. I was home on a deputation tour in the interests of the work
God had put in our hands in Argentina. This meeting was at the
old Bethany Baptist Church. The Sunday school auditorium and
classrooms at that time were on the first floor, with the church auditorium on the second. I had gone on ahead of the meeting to set
up my easel, and by chance I met Dad as he was slowly pulling
himself up those steep stairs, dragging one foot. I shall always
cherish the memory of his snow-white beard and the sparkle in
his eyes. Throughout the meeting he followed everything with
rapt interest.

When it was over he came forward, haltingly, and threw his
arms around my neck. With tears running down his cheeks he
said, "Son, keep on preaching the gospel as long as God gives you
breath."

These were his last words to his preacher son. His heart attack
came just a few days later, when I was in North Jersey. I was able
to drive down the turnpike five consecutive days to be at his bedside in the hospital until I had to return at night for missionary
rallies. We could not converse, because Dad, in his oxygen tent,
was too weak to talk; yet after his first attack, he was planning
how he would operate a tract ministry by mail from an invalid's
bed. Dad didn't know that half of his heart had been destroyed by
the attack; his one desire, to the very end, was to keep on serving
the Lord.

On the night of the memorial service, Harry Bollback, a veteran missionary, took my meeting for me in the New York area.

It is remarkable that the Lord allowed me to be in the United

States, both then and later on when Mother died. Each time I was in the general area, although every probability would have placed me five thousand miles away.

In the summer of 1969 I was on deputation tour with my son David, when my brother Dave's telephone call caught me at the Bible conference of the Ocean City Baptist Church. "Phil," Dave said, "if you want to see Mother alive you had better hurry."

We had been having conferences, both morning and evening; but the next morning, Saturday, was clear. Son David and I drove to Lancaster Valley over the fine superhighways and were at the house in about two hours. Dave's and Charlotte's children came spilling out of the door to greet us. We climbed the stairs to K-Ma's room.

Mother was terribly thin and wasted, unable to turn herself in bed. It was deeply touching to see the great love that Charlotte and Dave lavished on that precious, emaciated form; and they told us how the children brightened Mother's last weeks on earth with their brief visits.

My son David and I took chairs by her bed. Her gaunt chin was upthrust and her eyes were closed. Had we come too late? I took her frail, gnarled hand in mine. Ever so slowly she turned her head, and her large pale eyes opened.

"Momma, it's Philly. I've come to see you."

"Philly, my Philly . . ." The shadow of a smile appeared and faded.

"This is my boy David, Mother. He was just a little fellow when you saw him last, remember?"

Slowly, slowly Momma shifted her gaze to study David's features; then, apparently satisfied, she closed her eyes again. Her clawlike hand still clung to mine. I thought, "Is this all that is left of that strong body and sharply alert mind?" Physically, yes; but her wonderful spirit, untouched by infirmity, was still there, beside me! I began to relive some recent visits . . .

When I would phone her to say that I was coming by, her first thought was that I might be too tired, or too pressed. "Now, don't you come just for me," she would say, trying hard to sound convincing. "You just do your work for the Lord, and don't worry about your old mother."

What self-effacement! How she lost herself, thinking of the welfare and the needs of others! God knows how we need more mothers like her in the world.

Another time, "Now, Philly (my boyhood pet name), if you're too busy, don't feel that you have to bother phoning." That very day I was sitting beside her in the sunshine, stroking those dear, worn hands that had served us with such faithful love over the long years. . . . I recalled Mother's saying, some years back, that she prayed she would outlive Dad because, alone, he could never care for himself. She never wanted to be a burden or a bother to anyone, and after Dad went, she lived alone till within two months of her own homegoing. She had a little flag on a short mast outside her kitchen window, and each morning she raised it so that the good doctor who lived next door would know she was still alive.

Each time I arrived from the mission field, or from a deputation tour in the states, Mother would study my face intently. "Son, you are tired. You must not work so hard." And then, "Can I get you something to eat?"

Like a mother hen fluttering and clucking over a long-lost chick she would pad about in her shapeless dress and worn slippers, trying to do something to show the great love of her mother heart.

It was characteristic of her that, after she had blacked out and fallen crashing to the floor, smashing her dentures, she refused to have the plates replaced. "Nobody sees me anyway," she stoutly argued. "Besides, the money can go for missions."

Now our precious mother was tired, so very tired; but as she spoke from the bed, her words coming slow and separated, I felt the old spiritual warmth beneath them, like a coal fire banked for the night:

"Whatever I ask . . . of the Lord . . . He . . . always . . . gives me."

She must have asked Him for a peaceful departure from this war torn, sin-sick world; for she simply went to sleep one night, to wake up in the sweet presence of her beloved King, Jesus. And it may have been only coincidence, but from the time Mother died, trouble, deep trouble, began for the Aucas in the jungles of Ecuador where Rachel so faithfully ministered. Could it be that Mother's intercessory prayers had been holding back the forces of darkness, thousands of miles away?

Some years before her death, Mother had written:

"I cry aloud, and with all the strength of my soul, that the will of the Lord may be done in the life of my daughter and the Auca Indians . . . and then I sing the doxology.

"I ask myself if Nate's martyrdom and that of the other missionaries (with him) may suffice for 'our lesser Calvaries,' but of course I have no way of knowing.

"My great desire is to learn what God is going to do. Everything is in His all-powerful hands. He knows what will have to take place, according to His will. His Only Begotten Son had to die and shed His blood so that I might be saved.

"These are tremendous days for me. When I cried to the Lord in agony, saying that I would be willing to see my only daughter die under the spears of the Indians, I understood better what the mother of Jesus suffered at the foot of the Cross. If it is necessary that Rachel die in order that the Indians from downriver come to know the saving power of God, I am ready to pay this price."

"Whatever I ask of the Lord He always gives me."

Mother prayed constantly for her children and for their families. I know that she prayed for my life and work to be in the center of God's will; and I believe that He has been bringing this to pass through the years. Lately He has been answering my prayers in wonderful ways that I never dreamed.

Here in Argentina a new day brightens—a day of glorious, Spirit-filled revival—and I am inexpressibly grateful for the small share He has given me in it. Some doors have been closed to me here, but many new doors have opened. The great majority of our friends in the states have stood by us loyally. Some of them have not understood all that has taken place, but have felt confident that whatever did happen to us has been for the glory of God. I have been overwhelmed by the love and enthusiasm I found, both here and in the United States, in churches which are opening hearts and minds to the whole truth of the scriptures. Both new believers and established Christians are realizing that Christ does much more than offer them an escape from hell and a promise of heaven. They are experiencing salvation for their whole being. We preach a Savior Who is Lord of the believer's life—now; the Solver of problems, now; the Healer of diseases, now; the Christ Who meets all of our needs, now and forever.

By God's grace the Lake Valley Bible Conference Center continues to grow—a faith work that from the very start was conceived on a large scale. I believe God intends it to be a national and international center where believers will be empowered by His Holy Spirit for His work. Every year it is training more and more spiritual leaders to preach the full salvation God offers through His Son, salvation which transforms men into Jesus' own image, "even as by the Spirit of the Lord!" (II Cor. 3:18).

I believe that around this center of full-gospel testimony there will arise a Christian orphanage and a home for destitute widows. Perhaps God will make possible a Bible institute as well. All of the basic buildings are already there, except for a central auditorium and more dormitory space. Our Lake Valley property covers the equivalent of one hundred city blocks. We have already had as many as two hundred and seventy-five young people there in a single week.

As for myself, I believe that if the Lord tarries and allows me to continue in this work, the next years will be the most fruitful of my whole life. I feel that I am on the threshold of a more effective ministry than I have ever known. I feel younger in heart, even in body, than I did ten or fifteen years ago. By God's grace, until He calls me home, I shall continue to preach "the unsearchable riches of Christ," and the fullness that God has revealed to us by His Spirit (I Cor. 2:9–10).

I am drinking deeply of the Presence of the Lord Jesus, and oh, the abiding joy that floods my soul! Call it what you will—"the fullness of the Spirit," "the baptism in the Spirit," "the victorious Life"—this is what dominates the amazing revival now sweeping through Argentina. Its miracles of grace are all but incredible and can be explained in no other terms than the fulfillment of the prophecy of Joel: "In those days I shall pour out of my Spirit upon all flesh . . ."

If you wish to share in
Phil Saint's work write to:

> Spanish Evangelistic Crusades
> PHIL SAINT
> Box 1002
> Greensboro,
> North Carolina 27400
> U.S.A.

1   Me and my better half

2   K-Ma

3   Dad at work

4   On, or rather in, the road

5 *The Lord's movable house*

6 *And as many more, outside*

7 *Cordoba, aflame with revolution*

8   Nate

9   Curaray Beach

10   Giketa   11   Rachel and Dayuma

12   *Earthquake!*

13   *View from our camp*